PAL 709

VINCENT TWINS

P. Bickerstaff

CONTENTS

Foulis

Haynes

ISBN 0 85429 460 0

A FOULIS Motorcycling Book

First published 1984

© **Haynes Publishing Group**

Published by:
Haynes Publishing Group
Sparkford, Yeovil,
Somerset BA22 7JJ

Haynes Publications Inc.
861 Lawrence Drive, Newbury Park, California 91320, USA

British Library Cataloguing in Publication Data
Vincent Twins super profile.—
(Super profile)
   1. Vincent H.R.D. motorcycle
   I. Bickerstaff, Peter   II. Series
   629.28'775   TL448.V53
   ISBN 0–85429–460–0

Photographs: Andrew Morland and Author
Road tests: Motor Cycling courtesy of EMAP National Press Ltd

Printed in England by: J.H. Haynes & Co. Ltd

Titles in the *Super Profile* series

Ariel Square Four (F388)
BSA A7 & A10 (F446)
BMW R69 & R69/S (F387)
Brough Superior SS100 (F364)
BSA Bantam (F333)
Honda CB750 sohc (F351)
Matchless G3/L & G80 (F455)
MV Agusta America (F334)
Norton Commando (F335)
Sunbeam S7 & S8 (F363)
Triumph Bonneville (F453)
Triumph Thunderbird (F353)
Triumph Trident (F352)
KSS Velocette (F444)

Austin-Healey 'Frogeye' Sprite (F343)
Ferrari 250GTO (F308)
Fiat X1/9 (F341)
Ford Cortina 1600E (F310)
Ford GT40 (F332)
Jaguar E-Type (F370)
Jaguar D-Type & XKSS (F371)
Jaguar Mk 2 Saloons (F307)
Jaguar SS90 & SS100 (F372)
Lancia Stratos (F340)
Lotus Elan (F330)
MGB (F305)
MG Midget & Austin-Healey Sprite (except 'Frogeye') (F344)
Morris Minor Series MM (F412)
Morris Minor & 1000 (ohv) (F331)
Porsche 911 Carrera (F311)
Rolls-Royce Corniche (F411)
Triumph Stag (F342)

B29 Superfortress (F339)
Boeing 707 (F356)
Harrier (F357)
Jaguar (F438)
Mig 21 (F439)
Mosquito (F422)
Phantom II (F376)
P51 Mustang (F432)
Sea King (F377)
Super Etendard (F378)
Tiger Moth (F421)
Vulcan (F436)

Great Western Kings (F426)
Intercity 125 (F428)
V2 'Green Arrow' Class (F427).

FOREWORD

I do not remember how or when my appreciation of Vincents began, for I was only a child when they ceased production, but it was probably through my father, whose generation dreamed of being able to afford a new one. He finally obtained a very tired, but nevertheless reliable, Rapide in 1962, when prices were rock-bottom and the 'classic' revival was still in the future. Similarly, my own first Vincent was an abandoned pre-war single, salvaged off a scrap heap with the optimism of an apprentice; a number of years passed before it actually ran again. Eventually, my father relinquished the Rapide, and after a long, but skimpy, overhaul (still on student income) PUB 335 became mine.

My interest in vintage motorcycles is well known; a 1926 HRD serves me well in that role, but the Rapide is not kept as a hobby. PUB is my workaday transport, chosen in preference to any modern alternative in spite of a few acknowledged shortcomings. It has earned my respect over 150,000 miles of current day motorcycling, and so I think my judgement is not too clouded by 'looking back through rose coloured spectacles'. No small part of my enthusiasm for the marque can be attributed to the Vincent-HRD Owners Club, and the people with whom my bike brings me into contact. It is through the efforts of enthusiasts that a steady supply of spares and services continue to make running a Vincent regularly a practical proposition. Much more than that is the friendship which my Vincent-HRDs, and the VOC have generated for me. Through them I have rallied and been accommodated in Europe, Australia, Canada, and the USA, by people who greet me as a friend without ever having seen me before. The more one puts in, the greater seems to be the reward, and I am proud to be associated with the marque.

It is often said that 'character' is another word for unreliability in a motorcycle, but my most treasured machines are the most reliable ones. I prefer to believe that something personal, a part of the designer or a small team, is embodied in a machine which a computer or committee-designed 'consumer durable' never has. The genius of Phillip Vincent, and the engineering skills of Phil Irving, are there in a Vincent, to see and to feel by those with enough sensitivity to do so. I have even been lucky enough to meet these men in person.

I am pleased to have the opportunity to present this profile of the V-twins, but I am only writing it down. The information has come from many sources over a period of time. My thanks are due to many people who have helped me and taught me, from PCV and PEI through to acquaintances whose names I have not learned, but who have added little snippets of information. To try and make a list would be foolish, so this less specific acknowledgement of their help must suffice. I would, however, like to express my grateful thanks to Gordon Duerden and John Hurt who so willingly made their machines available for the photographs that appear in this book, and the interviewees, Frank Oliver, Alan Jennings and John Waltham for talking frankly about their bikes.

P. Bickerstaff

HISTORY

In 1921 Howard R. Davies, already a very successful racing man, established his place in the history books by becoming the only man to win a Senior TT on a Junior mount (a record which still stands technically), riding a Wolverhampton-built AJS. In 1925 he confirmed this place by winning the Senior TT on a mount of his own manufacture, less than a year since its launch. The HRD had arrived. At this time it too was built in Wolverhampton, with the help of some ex-AJS workers, to the same high standards as the other local marques which included the Sunbeam, with its renowned enamelwork. With sporting JAP engines and rigid frames, these HRDs had performance and handling to justify their high price, which makes them sought after vintage machines even today. Initially, they enjoyed considerable competition success, with a very healthy order book. The factory expanded to keep pace with demand, but with very little financial backing. As a result it was ill equipped to withstand the downturn in the prestige motorcycle market which occurred in the late twenties: not just because of the looming recession, but also because of some anti-motorcycle press arising from incidents such as the death of

Birkin during TT practice, which in those days was carried out on open roads. Even a second TT win, by Freddie Dixon in the 1927 Junior, was not enough to restore the factory's fortunes and so in February 1928 the motorcycle press reported that HRD Motors had been taken over by Ernie Humphries (of OK Supreme). The works were stripped, for Ernie had no intention of continuing production, at least not there and then.

Coincidentally, at the beginning of 1928, *The Motor Cycle* also carried an article about a new spring frame designed by a young undergraduate named Philip C Vincent. He had built the prototype in 1927, and armed with a patent and some backing from his father was intent on leaving University and setting up as a motorcycle manufacturer. To obtain a 'flying start' it seemed a good idea to try and acquire a well-respected trademark, and so for the sum of £500 the HRD name and a few remaining assets were passed on to 'PCV' as he became known. The new Vincent-HRD company set up their premises in Stevenage, where they remained thereafter. The company continued to use the HRD monogram, with just the addition of VINCENT in very small letters on the tank transfers. In spite of the flying start, PCV did not book any sales at his first Olympia show, although this was at least partly due to the unusual looks of these early Vincent-HRDs. From the very first prototype a 'triangulated swinging arm', which would now be referred to as a 'cantilever rear suspension' was fitted which did not look too different from the more usual rigid frame. However, on the early 'triangulated' frames the front section of frame was built on the same theme, which involved a pair of bracing tubes running across the engine in a very conspicuous manner. The public never got used to this strange look and sales remained very low until a more

conventional looking 'light frame' was introduced. This retained the rear suspension system of course, to become the standard frame, with slight modifications, through to 1939. Probably it had been fortunate that sales built up slowly, for in the recession many larger firms were unable to keep busy enough and were forced out of business, whereas the fledgeling Vincent-HRD company needed but few orders. One triangulated model which did make a mark for itself was a 600cc model E, which carried J. Gill, a passenger, and a sidecar full of luggage around the world in 1929/30. Not only was this good publicity, but the passenger changed in Australia; and the man who came back to England was a talented engineer who was to have a decided influence on the future Vincent-HRDs, and a number of other marques too. His name was P.E. Irving.

Of the many features developed over the years, rear suspension was the first. A problem which this brought in its wake was that of seating the passenger. The normal pad mounted on the rear mudguard was even less comfortable on the Vincent, but a fully sprung arrangement could overload the friction-damped springing, and also look unsightly, which was a mistake the factory did not wish to repeat. The solution was a half-sprung scheme, neatly achieved by using a pair of unobtrusive, but scientifically placed links, supporting the rear of the seat directly from the rear frame. This was introduced in 1933, which year also saw the first 'duo-brakes' fitted, another distinctive Vincent feature. PCV reasoned that a brake on each side of a wheel distributed loads symmetrically for truer steering whilst braking, and provided much more area for heat dissipation to avoid brake fade. The resulting brakes proved good enough to cope with the performance of later 1000cc machines, with only detailed attention to drum and lining materials.

Until 1934 Vincent-HRDs were all fitted with proprietary engines, Rudge 'Python' units gradually ousting the JAPs in popularity. This was true also inside the factory, when the special racing JAP engines let the works bikes down badly in the 1934 TT. As a result the company decided to go ahead with their own engines, and models fitted with the new units were on show at Olympia in 1934. Just as the first frame laid down the principles for those that were to follow, so this first engine design carried many of the features which would become 'trademarks' in the later designs. The most noticeable of these was the layout of the valve gear. The camshaft was fitted high in the crankcases, driven by a large idler (known in the period as semi-overhead camshaft, a term which fell into disuse to avoid confusion with single overhead camshaft). The short pushrods were widely splayed, in line with the valves, and a further reduction in pushrod length was gained by using forked rockers bearing on a collar low down on the valve. The valve gear was enclosed, but the arrangement permitted the top of the valve stem and the springs to be outside in the cool air. The whole engine was kept short, like the Rudge 4-valve units it replaced. This itself was a useful feature, for the tall JAPs necessitated a little door in the side of the petrol tank in order to gain access to their tappets! Within a year the new engine proved its robustness and performance by powering Jack Williams and Noel Christmas to seventh and ninth places respectively in the 1935 Senior TT, ahead of older JAP-engined models which took eleventh, twelfth, and thirteenth places.

Proprietary engined models were dropped, and instead a range of models used the new engine, but with different specifications. The Meteor was bottom of the range; in 1937 it was listed at £89.10.0

when a Rudge 'Ulster' cost £82 and Pride & Clarke could offer a 500cc Cotton for only £44. Vincents were never cheap! At £96, the Comet model was a little more luxurious, with its stainless steel panelled tank, and in a slightly higher state of tune. Racers would buy the TT replica if they could find the £118 asking price. For a time it was possible to buy a hot-stuff roadster in the form of the bronze-headed TT replica engine housed in road-going Comet cycle parts, but PCV did not favour this approach because the customer might have difficulty maintaining tune for full performance. Phil Irving stumbled upon a better idea one day when looking through jig and engine drawings, for he noticed that if a cylinder angle of 47 degrees were chosen, the factory could machine a V-twin with much of its existing equipment. It would, of course, use the same barrels, heads, and valve gear as the singles, and quite a lot of the bottom end too, whilst the strong TT Replica frame would house the twin with just a slightly lengthened top-tube. Thus was born the first Series 'A' Rapide. Anything but a very softly tuned sidecar-tug, it proved to be a high performance mount with a top speed of 110mph as standard, and capable of lapping Brooklands at the magic 'ton'. Jim Kentish did just that to gain his Gold Star on this famous circuit. Weight was kept

within reasonable bounds by using alloy barrels, and the alloy-composite brakes of the racing models (two per wheel of course was standard practice). The Rapide could also boast great flexibility, as the normal state of tune was only to the lowest 'Meteor' level. Even in this trim the Achilles heel, a weak transmission, showed itself so that the manufacturers of the Burman gearbox had to make gears in a stronger steel and the owners handbook warned against using full throttle before the clutch was fully home and biting. It was inevitable therefore that racing versions could have only a limited success. Nevertheless, the factory built one works model with which Ginger Wood broke the Donington lap record, and a few others were prepared to order. The whole production run was only about 80 machines because the price was high – £142 in 1937 – and in only three years the coming of war brought a halt.

Exactly what the specification of a Series 'A' Rapide is would be hard to say, for they would so often be made to customer specification and supplied direct. Whilst the early specification mentioned alloy heads, they were never fitted to anything except some works singles. The comment applies to a lesser extent to the other models, because it was a small firm, quite willing to adapt to customer needs, or indeed to supply conditions. At various times pre-war they tried water-cooled two-strokes, enclosure, and a delivery three-wheeler. Other efforts to keep the works busy included motorcycle reconditioning work, and during the period of selling direct to the public they handled a few New Imperials too (a firm who were licensed to use the Vincent seat mounting arrangement on their own spring frame models). In the latter part of the thirties they undertook contract work on munitions, as the build up of arms began.

When war broke out, motorcycle production stopped, for

other factories such as BSA and Matchless were much better able to mass produce WD machines. Instead, the Vincent-HRD works turned over to producing mines and shells, and then aircraft parts. With the fertile brain of Phil Vincent, the engineering skill of Phil Irving and an engine test house all deprived of motorcycles to develop, it was perhaps inevitable that they would think of something else to work on. PCV managing to be in the right place at the right time obtained a contract to develop an engine for an airborne lifeboat (something which would be carried out to sea by air, and dropped to survivors who would then find their own way home). Power required was quite low, the propeller could only cope with 15bhp, and water would be readily available for cooling, but the engine had to be light and very economical on fuel. It will surprise many to find that PCV turned successfully to a two-stroke to achieve this objective. It was, however, no ordinary two-stroke, but a 'Uniflow' design featuring two opposed pistons in each cylinder, one controlling inlet and the other exhaust. Each had a crankshaft, but they ran a little out of step to achieve asymmetric port timing. Actually there were two such cylinders, displacing 500cc total, with a charging cylinder between them, containing two double acting cast-iron pumping pistons, and crossheads. With three cylinders and six pistons it was really a 'four'! A change of heart about methods of air-sea rescue meant that only a very few of these engines, or their derivatives, were made, and in turn put an end to plans to develop a motorcycle and a small car (with front wheel drive and transverse engine) having the same features. In the little spare time that existed between these tasks, PCV and PEI were planning the motorcycle which they would build after the war, for they were not content merely to resurrect their pre-war model range.

There was no doubt in their minds that the Series 'A' Rapide was the right kind of bike, nor that the special Vincent features such as rear suspension, high cam valve gear, etc. should remain. On the other hand the transmission had undoubtedly proved inadequate, and the stretched frame was longer in the wheelbase than desirable. With its external oil-pump, four feedpipes, four rocker oilpipes, sundry petrol pipes, and prominent exhaust pipes, the pre-war model had gained the nickname 'Plumbers Nightmare' and the designers wished to be rid of that tag. The oil pump was moved inside, and drillings used to convey lubricant with just the feed and return pipes to the tank being external, passing the rockers neatly by on the way. The only solution for the transmission was to redesign it, in unit with the engine, for rigidity and clean lines. A multiplate clutch was not considered satisfactory and so the Vincent ingenuity was put to work resulting in the very misunderstood 'self-servo' clutch which is **NOT** centrifugal. Rather a conventional, but light, clutch transmits low power but simultaneously operates a drum clutch (just like a drum brake) which transmits most of the power. More ingenuity was needed to stiffen and shorten the frame. It resulted in $3\frac{1}{2}$ inch diameter front and rear downtubes, more recognisable as the front and rear cylinders! This way they neither added weight nor size over and above the engine. The top tube was bolted up to the cylinder heads, fabricated in large rectangular section and used also as the oil tank. A fairly similar rear triangle to the pre-war one completed the frame, pivoted from the back of the gearbox. Aluminium alloys for the cylinders, heads, mudguards, and various other parts kept the weight down, in spite of the very sturdy construction, and also kept the steel content low, which was quite important in the steel-starved post-war years. Indeed the strange multi-spring engine shaft shock

absorber of the Vincent was designed that way as much because of steel availability as for technical reasons; because the pre-war model had had a rubber device in the clutch, Vincents got no allocation of thick spring wire! Aluminium alloy production had greatly increased during the war years, and with no continuing need for aeroplanes, it was relatively easy to obtain. A year or two later, when designing their own front fork, Vincents chose light alloy again for the main blades, a tough and heat treated alloy being selected. The resulting motorcycle boasted a weight of 450lbs, a wheelbase of 56 inches, and a seat height of 30 inches. Whilst the advertisements 'light as a TT 500' may have overstated the achievement, a little hindsight shows that the journalists common tag of a 'leviathan' was hardly justified, for few big bikes of the 70s and 80s are anything like so small. The first prototype was assembled early in 1946, and given a test run by Graham Walker of *Motor Cycling* the following day. This showed either tremendous faith in the design, or the not uncommon small firm problem of having to work flat out to honour promises made in advance.

Early commercial success was restricted by the numbers which the factory could build; the buyers were there but the automatic production machinery was not. The numbers turned out were small, and so too therefore were profits, something which, within a few years, turned into a crisis. Those which could be turned out were very enthusiastically received, not the least for speed work. In road racing the opportunities were limited, 500cc being the grand prix limit, although airfield races for 1000cc machines did take place. For a few years there was a 1000cc Clubmans TT. Riders such as George Brown (then road racing) soon proved the winning abilities of the model, and changed opinion from 'much too big and heavy to be any good' into cries of 'unfair to use 1000cc'. George raced a number of works machines very successfully, including a 500cc hybrid, an amalgamation of pre- and post-war design, known as the Cadwell Special. Its name was derived from its success at that circuit, winning the Folbigg trophy a number of times. The first and most famous factory twin, 'Gunga Din' started life as a reject Rapide, to become a testbed for the sports and racing models that were to follow, and a successful racer and record breaker winning on airfields, such as Silverstone, putting up the fastest time at hillclimbs like Shelsley Walsh, and breaking the 5km sidecar record in the hands of Rene Milhoux. Indeed it is in the fields of sprinting and record breaking that Vincents had their greatest competition success. George Brown himself eventually set up his own business, across the road from the works in Stevenage, and proceeded to develop Nero (built from a burnt out wreck) and Super Nero (supercharged), his own Vincents. These became more specialised for hillclimbs and then sprinting, so that for twenty years George was the man to beat in those sports. The other 'sport' in which the Vincent made its biggest mark was record breaking. The advertising boast *The World's Fastest Standard Motorcycle* was indeed a fact and not just a slogan, for a number of customers in the early post-war years found they could wheel out the new bike and promptly capture National records with it. Thus encouraged, some owners began tuning for higher honours, and met with considerable success. Some of the later machines started life at the factory, prepared as the racing variant, the Black Lightning, but many started as humble Rapides. Col Crothers took the Australian record to 145mph on Lake Eyre. Bob Burns in New Zealand started his record breaking with a British Empire sidecar record of 146mph on a

second-hand Rapide. He then teamed up with Russell Wright with a new (1953) Black Lightning. Using the Ohaka Tram Road in New Zealand, this pair put up absolute World's records of 155mph (sidecar, Burns in December 1954) and 162mph (solo, Wright, July 1955). When NSU raised the figures again, the pair prepared an attack at Bonneville in 1956. There Burns got the sidecar figure up to 175mph, which was enough, although eventually the FIM refused to ratify them because they did not authorise the timing gear. Wright could only reach 196mph, which was not enough by then for a solo record. Even into the 80s record breaking continues. At Bonneville in 1980 Dave Matson took two class records on petrol at 175mph (approx), and in 1981 produced timed runs at over 200mph with nitro, although not making runs in the opposite direction, necessary to claim a record. The factory's own record attempt, made at Montlhéry, was a mixed success. They were after the 24 hour record, but the standard big end fitted did not hold out, failing after 11 hours. Records were bagged over shorter times and distances, 100mph plus up to 6 hours, and 99mph to 10 hours. Gunga Din also just failed to take short distance records, at around 150mph, because the heat and speed kept lifting off the tyre treads.

Naturally the public wanted sports and racing versions. Fuel at this time (1948) was still 'Pool' of only 72 octane, well below even modern 2-star, and so a slight increase in compression ratio to 7.3 was the limit before unacceptable pinking set in. Slightly larger carburettor sizes, polished and selected internals, stiffer ribbed brake drums, and a few other modifications improved both the go and the stop. To give a distinctive image, the new model was given a fairly radical all-black heat dispersing finish to its engine and a

corresponding name – the Black Shadow. With a target speed of 125mph (road tests varied from 122mph to 128mph) this was the highest performance offered by a normal road-going motorcycle for 20 years. Not that too many motorcyclists could actually have one; all machines were hard to get in the early post-war years, and Vincents were expensive too. The Rapide cost £361 in 1950, and the Black Shadow £425. For comparison, a Triumph Thunderbird of that period was listed at £194. By this time the range had been broadened with the introduction of the Series C cycle-parts (Girdraulic fork and hydraulic damping), with the 500cc models using the 1000cc cycle parts, and general layout, but with separate engine and Burman gearbox/clutch. Corresponding to the twin cylinder touring Rapide, sports Black Shadow, and racing Black Lightning models, their 500cc equivalents were the Meteor (relatively few built, in Series B form only), Comet (Series C) and Grey Flash (Series C, but available in a variety of trims, from stripped to fully road equipped). Even the 500cc Comet was priced at £273. Coincidental with the change from Series B to Series C, the old HRD monogram was dropped in favour of Vincent alone, on the engine and crankcases, because in the American market HRD tended to be confused with Harley-Davidson as indeed still happens to this day. Most 'B's are HRDS and most 'C's are Vincents, but it is not always so.

The post-war models were very successful in motorcycling terms, but commercially the situation was not so good. Shortages of materials and machine tools had kept production low, too low to cover overheads effectively, and by mid-1949 the factory was in serious financial trouble. The bankers called in a receiver and it looked very much like the end. However, Mr E.C. Baillie, who was the man called in, decided that there was scope for recovery. New machinery came in, and the pricing structure was adjusted to suit the works capacity, so that by 1952 the firm was sound enough to be reconstituted as Vincent Engineers (Stevenage) Ltd. It should therefore be remembered that most of the Vincents built were built in receivership or shortly afterwards! Mr Baillie remains an honorary member of the Vincent club to this day for his efforts. One surprising result of this financial trouble was an entry in the 1950 Senior TT. Very few British factories have made official entries post-war, but the Receiver saw this as a very good way of advertising that the Vincent-HRD company was remaining in business. A limited amount of development work was put in on the new Grey Flash model and four were prepared for the Island. In the event three retired, but the fourth, ridden by Ken Bills who stood in for an injured George Brown, finished twelfth at 84mph. Compared with the 92mph of winner Geoff Duke, and their own previous best of 75mph, this was a quite creditable performance.

An even more creditable feat, which is surely unique to the marque, was the 100,000 mile road test undertaken privately by Tony Rose, in 16 months from November 1951. That represented a tremendous feat of endurance for the rider, as well as the machine. It was intended to complete the test without ever opening up the engine, but in the rush to the works for the half way check-up, an oil pipe broke and went unnoticed! Tony was all for continuing, but was prevailed upon to lift the barrels, where broken piston rings were found and replaced. The report by Cyril Quantrill contains a serious error in stating that this had occurred at one third distance, probably due to confusion over the replacement of rocker bushes on that occasion. It seems Cyril may not have realised that on a Vincent the rocker gear can be withdrawn through the inspection cap. The

emphasis on 'no carbon was removed' serves to remind readers that in the 1950s decoking was normal practice every few thousand miles, and a part of the test was to prove that a Vincent run on *Filtrate* oil did not require this archaic practice.

Luxury motorcycle production was a precarious business, made more so as the post-war boom began to tail off, and building engines in small numbers is expensive. Vincents examined and tried a number of ways to diversify and to increase production. Using the twin engine, a prototype 3-wheeler was built, a prototype 'Vindian' was made (with a Vincent engine in an American-style Indian frame, Indian at that time being US importers), and a few engines were supplied for car racing. A similar 'Picador' engine was developed for a target aircraft, a small batch of these 70bhp engines being built. However none of these avenues came to fruition so the motorcycle activity had to be self-supporting. Other work in the factory included the manufacture of a bicycle 'clip-on' engine, the Firefly, which was made in many thousands for a time, but became obsolete when Vincents themselves imported the far superior NSU Quickly moped. Other NSU lightweights (98cc ohv and 123cc two-stroke) were made up with a large proportion of British components in order to meet

import taxation rules. These arrangements too were fairly short-lived, and NSU reverted to more direct importing. A line of work which did become the mainstay of the Vincent business was small industrial and marine engines. These were designed in 75cc and 100cc two-stroke single sizes, but could also be coupled up as twins. They were used in lawnmowers, compressors, inboard and outboard marine work, even go-karting. A few ideas for moped/scooter/ motorcycle variants were tried but never proceeded with. A fibreglass water scooter fitted with this engine was manufactured, but it was the failure of this venture (apparently due to an unsatisfactory grade of fibreglass from a sub-contractor) which finally brought the firm down in 1958. It was sold to Harper Engines, and in turn acquired by Cope Allman International. The Vincent name and assets were then sold to Matt Holder, and on his death have passed to his son David. But long before all this, motorcycle production had ceased (although not the manufacture of spares which continued for 20 years).

The Series 'D' was the last of the Vincent twins (only one or two singles were made) when in 1955, both engine and frame were revised. After consultation with the owners club, some weak points were improved, such as the use of coil ignition for easier starting, a more robust engine shock absorber etc. Other manufacturers had finally caught up with rear suspension, so this too was improved by having longer travel, using proprietary dampers (Armstrong), and featuring fully sprung seating. This was all below the surface, and at the 1954 Show it was the skin which drew attention, for the bikes featured all-enveloping fibreglass panelling, legshields, and windscreens. Known as the Black Knight and Black Prince, respectively, these models were to replace their older Rapide and Black Shadow counterparts. Suppliers and

customers however dictated otherwise. Good quality mouldings proved to be slow in coming, such that only 200 enclosed Vincents rolled off the line. Once again PCV found motorcyclists too conservative to accept his ideas. Although the whole motorcycling world thought enclosure was the way for future development, the buying public thought otherwise. Prompted by the FIM ban on full streamlining in racing, the motorcycle soon returned to its old naked state, and in 1984 motorcycles batter their way

through the air in the same crude fashion as they had done in 1894, when Hildebrand and Wolfmuller put the first practical motorcycle on the market. For the Vincent factory the demand for naked models meant revised and not very pretty subframes were used for the fully sprung seating on the new 'D' specification Rapide and Black

Shadow models. But motorcycle production continued to prove uneconomic, and at the end of 1955 the last Vincent motorcycle rolled off the production line.

EVOLUTION

The Rapide was introduced at the 1936 Olympia show, for the 1937 season. It was based on the 500cc singles, with a similar tubular frame, separate engine and gearbox, rear-springing and duo-brakes. In the interest of lightness, some racing parts were often fitted such as alloy cylinder barrels and brakeplates, but not the alloy heads listed, for these only ever appeared on a few 'works' singles. Ignition and lighting was by Lucas 'Magdyno', a special $47\frac{1}{2}$ degree instrument to suit the odd cylinder angle, and mounted inverted, at the front. Engines were normally in a low state of tune, in deference to the transmission, but some with polished internals and racing cams were made. Finish was usually black with gold lining and many fittings in stainless steel. Speedometer and a matching 8-day clock were standard fittings. Only 80 of the pre-war Rapides were built.

The post-war Rapide was an extensively redesigned model, but nevertheless drawing on the experience and structure of its predecessor. Thus it retained the bore and stroke of 84x90mm, and the valve gear layout of high gear-driven camshafts operating the valves through short, splayed, pushrods and forked rockers. Magneto ignition from a similarly placed instrument was retained, with gear instead of chain drive. The transmission was a robust Vincent design, built-in unit with the engine for strength and cleanliness. A triplex primary chain, tensioned with an adjustable blade, drove through the unique Vincent self-servo clutch. The operating lever only lifted a light conventional clutch, this in turn operating two shoes in a drum to transmit the majority of power through well-cooled parts. Action tends to be fierce, and the unit was never made tolerant of oil so that a separate dry chamber had to be provided which added to the width where the footrests are sited. Extensive use of alloys, for cylinder heads and barrels (with cast-iron liners) offset the extra weight in the transmission to some extent. The novel frame, or more exactly lack of frame, aided weight reduction. The oil tank/spine bolted to the top of the engine carried the Brampton girder forks, and the rear suspension attached directly to the power unit. A dualseat was also a novelty, but simplified the saddle/pillion support considerably. 50 watt Miller lighting was the best available in 1946, and Amal carburettors were almost the only choice for a motorcycle. Early models had carburettors that were difficult to adjust because there were no left-handed ones for the front cylinder. These were fitted when available, in brass at first, until demand was sufficient for Amal to tool up for zinc based diecastings. For post-war 'Pool' petrol of 72 octane, the standard compression ratio was 6.8:1, or lower if compression plates were specified.

Development led to the introduction of the Black Shadow (also known occasionally and confusingly as the 'Rapide Black Shadow model' or 'Black Shadow sports model Rapide') in February 1948. Externally the changes were ribbed brake drums for stiffer action and better heat dissipation, a black painted power unit, and carburettors of $1\frac{1}{8}$inch instead of the Rapide's $1\frac{1}{16}$inch. Internally, the compression ratio was raised to 7.3:1, parts were polished, and the selection of parts on the production line ensured that Shadows had slightly longer valve timings, and marginally different big-end clearances. Triple valve springs were specified for a time but proved to be of no advantage so a reversion was made to the double arrangement. The 'piece de resistance' was the fitting of a 5inch diameter speedometer, prominently displaying to the world a calibration to 150mph because the normal 120mph spread was inadequate.

Standard specification for all models included aluminium mudguards, straight handlebars and 20inch diameter front and 19inch diameter rear wheels, but for North and South America, an alternative version was produced. Initially it was available to special order, then offered as 'Export' specification, and finally as 'Touring' specification, to be available on all models, at home as well as abroad. The differences comprised 19inch front and 18inch rear wheels, with an extra $\frac{1}{2}$inch tyre section to improve comfort whilst maintaining the same rolling diameter, big, valanced, steel mudguards, and raised 'cow horn' handlebars. Comfort on rough roads improved at the expense of a little extra weight and slightly heavier steering. The option was available from 1948 to 1954.

The majority of machines were built, or converted, to Series 'C' specification. This Series first became available in 1948, but did not supersede the Series 'B' until 1950 when supplies of the new parts became freely available. Primarily, this change in specification consisted of fitting the factory's own 'Girdraulic' fork in place of the girders at the front, but advantage was taken of the opportunity to fit the hydraulic damper at the rear too, to assist the friction damping. Other manufacturers were changing to telescopic forks but PCV and Phil Irving disliked the flexibility of those, due to very poor bracing between the two sides. Instead they redesigned the girder layout, with forged alloy blades pinned together by the spindles, and long, one piece links for rigidity and longer movement than the Bramptons. The soft action of the telescopics was matched by using long side springs, and a single hydraulic damper in the central position usually occupied by a girder fork spring. Sidecar outfits were a common form of transport then (for which telescopics are particularly poorly suited) and so the new fork was made adjustable such that a simple bit of spannerwork reset the spring preload and fork trail for sidecar work. Different springs and a proprietary damper were adopted for the Series 'D' models, but otherwise this fork was retained on all subsequent models until production ceased.

When the Series 'D' range reintroduced the Rapide and Black Shadow models, the basic specification remained the same, but there were many detailed alterations. Touring wheel sizes became standard, 60 watt Lucas electrics with coil ignition replaced the magneto and Miller lighting, one rear brake was omitted, and the dualseat became fully sprung instead of mounted on links to the rear frame member. The major engine changes comprised adopting the same cylinder head for front and rear (it has never been made clear why they were made different in the first place), Amal Monobloc carburettors, and an atmospheric breathing system instead of the previous timed arrangement. Underneath their skirts, the enclosed models were also to this specification.

Various efforts have been made to reintroduce Vincents, most notably the Egli-Vincents of the 1970s, and recently new castings made by the Holder family. As an outstanding machine of the 1946/8 era, perhaps it is as well that it should remain unchanged.

Summary of model changes

Engine modifications

	Engine number
	(F10AB/1.. = Rapide)
	(F10AB/1B.. = Black Shadow)
3 inch dynamo replaces 3½inch, altered clutch seal etc.	1300
Bronze or alloy breather sleeve, steel pinion	1400
Altered gearchange camplate contours	1590
Grooved rocker bearings, to improve oil drainage	2340
Steel oil pump worm	2991
Vincent embossed crankcases	3090
Self-hardening stainless steel pushrods	3132
Low clearance pistons	3716
Alloy large idler, replacing bronze for quietness	4548
Triple valve springs (Shadow models) dropped	5336
Low (Rapide) bottom gear adopted on Black Shadow	7076
Mark 3 cams with quietening ramps	8343
Modified gearchange (limit stops)	8500/8700
Oil restrictor discs fitted in timing cover	9238
Stellite tipped clutch actuating lever	9701
Revised timing cover drillings, no restrictor discs	10,000
Divided clutch pushrod, and ball bearing	10,021

Frame modifications

	Frame Number
	R...... = B Rapide
	R...... B = B Black Shadow
	RC... = C Rapide
	RC... B = C Black Shadow
Petrol tank tie bolt fitted to prevent splitting	2416
Cast iron adopted for brake drums, instead of steel	3050
Hydraulic rear damper	3500
Rear chain oiler with needle valve in oil tank neck	3800
Rear fork centres increased to 18 inch	3900
Steering headlug altered with matching head bracket	8614
Steering damper altered to two plate design	11,937

SPECIFICATION

Engine:	Rapide	Black Shadow
Capacity and bore and stroke	998cc	(84x90mm, 50° V-twin)
Compression ratio	6.8:1	7.3:1
Claimed bhp	45 @ 5300rpm	55 @ 5700rpm
Valve timing	Inlet opens 40/42° BTDC, closes 60/64° ABDC	
	Exhaust opens 70/72° BBDC, closes 28/33° ATDC	
Ignition timing	39° (13/64in) BTDC	38° (15/32in) BTDC
Magneto	Lucas KVF, contact breaker gap 0.012in	
Carburettors	2x Amal 276 ($1\frac{1}{16}$ in)	2xAmal 279 ($1\frac{1}{8}$ in)
Primary drive	Triplex 0.375in pitch chain, screw tensioner	

Wheelbase	$56\frac{1}{2}$ inch
Frame	Steel backbone (carrying oil), stressed engine
Suspension: front	Series 'B', friction-damped Brampton girders
	Series 'C' hydraulically-damped Vincent 'Girdraulic'
rear	Triangulated swinging arm, supported on taper-roller bearings, friction damping, with additional hydraulic damping on Series 'C' machines 6in travel
Wheels: front	3.00 x 20in (3.50 x 19in touring spec.) quickly detachable
rear	3.50 x 19in (4.00 x 18in touring spec.) quickly detachable
Tyres	Front: Avon 'Speedster' ribbed. Rear: Avon 'Supreme' block tread
Brakes	Dual 7x$\frac{7}{8}$ in, detachable drums on each wheel with fitted water excluders. Balanced front actuation. Ribbed brake drums on Black Shadow models
Final drive chain and sprockets	$\frac{3}{8}$ x $\frac{5}{8}$ in, 46t standard, options from 45 to 60 teeth, and for twin sprockets on the reversible wheel
Gear ratios	Top 3.5; 3rd 4.2; 2nd 5.6; 1st 9.1
	(Early Black Shadows 1st 7.2)
Lighting	Miller 50 watt D6 dynamo, driven off primary chain. 7in light unit and 13ah 'Exide' battery. (Early models had $3\frac{1}{2}$in D9S dynamo and 8in light)
Capacities: oil	6 Imp. pints
petrol	$3\frac{1}{4}$ Imp. gallons
Dry weight	455lbs (Rapide) 458lbs (Black Shadow) plus 15lbs when to 'Touring' specification
Terminal speed	Rapide :110mph; Black Shadow :125mph
Cruising speed	85mph and 100mph respectively
Consumption quoted	Petrol 55-65mpg, oil 200mpp
Equipment and finish	Enamelled parts 'Bonderised' and finished in Pinchin Johnson's best cycle enamel. (Black as standard, but Chinese Red was supplied to the US market). Bright parts polished stainless steel or aluminium, others chromium or cadmium plated. Feridax seat, Smiths speedometer. Rear stand, left and right prop-stands (which also lower together to raise the front wheel). Tool kit including tyre inflator, grease gun and tyre levers

ROAD TESTS

The 998 c.c. Twin o.h.v. (Series "C")

VINCENT "RAPIDE"

and

BLACKNELL

"SHERWOOD" SIDECAR

An o.h.v. Big Twin and Luxury Saloon Sidecar Give "Motor Cycling" Testers Fresh Ideas on Passenger Machine Averages and Maxima

A connoisseur's combination! The Series "C" Vincent "Rapide" attached to a Blacknell saloon sidecar.

WHAT is a reasonable cruising speed for a two-seater sidecar outfit? Fifty? Fifty-five, perhaps? Even a mile a minute if an over-500 c.c. motor is providing the power? Or What?

Motor Cycling decided to test a Vincent in sidecar trim and—because Blacknell Sidecars, Ltd., of Nottingham, have produced a range of chassis and bodies particularly adapted for use with a machine, such as the Vincent, with swinging arm rear suspension—a child-adult "Sherwood" saloon, mounted on the standard "Safety" chassis, was specified to be hitched to a touring "Rapide," with deep-section mudguards and "fat" tyres (3.50-in. by 19-in. front and 4.00-in by 18-in. rear).

The outfit has been "on the strength" for six months now, during which time it has covered some 4,000 miles, and—unless calamity intervenes in the form of a telephone call from Stevenage demanding its return—the "barouche," as it has come to be known, will be out again next week-end, on a duty trip or taking a "free" member of the staff and his family on a pleasure run.

Being no newcomer to the market, the "Rapide" needs only a brief description. Its massive 998 c.c. power unit is nowadays the only British example of what is often described as "the sidecarrist's ideal"—an o.h.v. vee-twin "thousand." Its high camshaft, short push-rod layout enables the engine to run at a much higher r.p.m. than usual with this type and a highly efficient dry-sump lubrication system and the use of light alloy for the cylinders and heads overcome that old bugbear of big twins—overheating on the rear cylinder. Separate Amal carburetters are fitted, with a cable junction box providing compensated control for the throttle opening and separate levers enabling individual settings to be given for each air slide.

The Lucas magneto has automatic advance

and retard mechanism and one of the very few criticisms which can be made of the machine is of the inability of the automatic device to compete with the special requirements of sidecar work—a weakness evidenced by pinking when accelerating sharply on hills.

A separate 50-watt Miller dynamo and voltage control unit, and a 13-amp.-hr. Exide battery attend to the lighting and warning equipment. The Miller head lamp furnishes a broad beam which makes night driving a pleasure and high praise goes to the Lucas "Altette" horn, which has a note which without being frightening, nevertheless gives distinctly audible warning of approach—a most necessary adjunct to a machine which is extremely quiet when running at 50 m.p.h. or less in top.

In semi-unit construction, the four-speed gearbox provides ratios ideally spaced for sidecar work and, additionally, there is a choice of rear sprockets which—compared with the more usual tooth-to-tooth change of engine sprocket—gives a far finer selection of gears. After running the road test outfit for a time with a 56-tooth sprocket—which gave a speedometer maximum of over 90 m.p.h. under favourable conditions—it was decided that a more suitable top-gear performance could be obtained by "cogging down"—in fact, adding teeth by fitting a 60-tooth sprocket.

(Below) The sidecar has a good streamline contour, which materially assists high-speed driving. Access to the rear locker is from inside the body.

But too great an accent must not be placed on sheer performance, for quite the most endearing attribute of the Vincent is its ability to gobble up miles effortlessly. Such is the manner in which the " Rapide " surmounts gradients without giving any indication that they even exist, such is its stopping power, and so well does it sweep round bends, that comfortable 35 m.p.h. averages can be maintained with the needle seldom going past the " 60 " mark.

Petrol consumption could be fairly heavy. There have been occasions when no more than 33 m.p.g. has ben recorded. Shocking? Hardly, for that figure has been coupled with a " 40 plus " average, on journeys of 150 or 200 miles. At the nominal figure of a maintained 30 m.p.h.—but who in his right senses wants to maintain a steady thirty on the Vincent outfit?—the consumption figure rises to 55 m.p.g.

Much the same variation comes in on oil consumption. When the machine is driven really hard—as it has been almost continually since it has been with *Motor Cycling*—a one-pint replenishment every second fill-up (every 220 to 250 miles on 3-gallon replenishments) has been normal, yet, when the outfit has been driven sedately for an equivalent distance—as when used for daily 16-mile

(Left) A phase in the exploratory run to Goodwood undertaken by "Motor Cycling" staff. The photographer forsook the sidecar momentarily to get this picture in the heart of Winchester, with the King Alfred memorial in the background

With that modification the actual ratios available are 4.56, 5.47, 7.3 and 12.5 to 1. That means a top-gear range of anything from 30 m.p.h. up to 80 m.p.h.—and up to that speed in a mere 31 sec.—without any changing down or lying flat. If the intermediate ratios are used, the jump from 30 m.p.h. to the same figure can be accomplished in as little as 21 sec., whilst the all-out, sitting-up-in-a-great-big-riding-coat maximum is just short of 80 m.p.h. with a passenger weight of one wife and two small children aboard, and the really getting-down-to-it figure with a single passenger is no less than 85 m.p.h.

Galloping the outfit with an empty sidecar, an 88 m.p.h. maximum figure has been recorded, allowing for 5 per cent. speedometer error. When obtaining the figures recorded on the tester's sheet, it was discovered that the change from second gear to third was none too simple and more than once " miscogging " resulted in fabulous—and frightening—surges of r.p.m.

With so much power available, an immediate thought is " do the brakes work? "

They do. There are four of them, two to each wheel of the machine and each of 7-in. diameter and, provided they are adjusted at fairly regular intervals—for halting 700 lb. of motorcycle and sidecar, plus about 3 cwt. of passengers, is no light duty—they will stop the combination in a distance which few sidecar outfits could equal. The limiting factors, in fact, are road surface and tyre adhesion—not the brake linings or leverage.

(Below) Although it is a two-seater, the Blacknell "Sherwood" by no means dwarfs the machine to which it is attached.

MOTOR CYCLING SPORTS MODEL ROAD TESTS

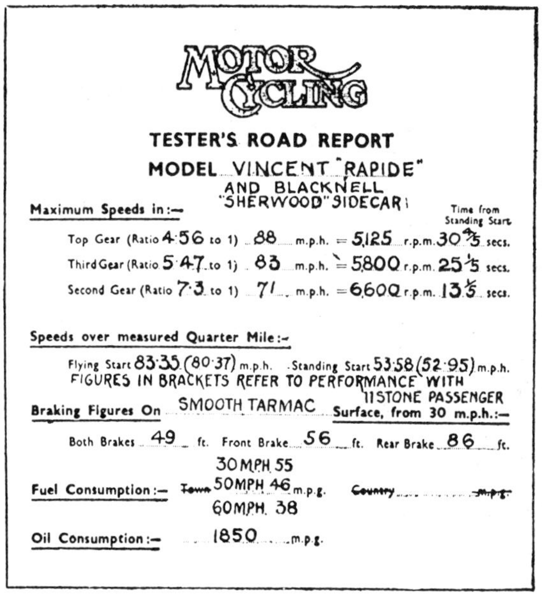
MOTOR CYCLING

TESTER'S ROAD REPORT

MODEL VINCENT "RAPIDE" AND BLACKNELL "SHERWOOD" SIDECAR

Maximum Speeds in:— Time from Standing Start

Top Gear (Ratio 4·56 to 1) 88 m.p.h. = 5,125 r.p.m. 30$\frac{4}{5}$ secs.

Third Gear (Ratio 5·47 to 1) 83 m.p.h. = 5,800 r.p.m. 25$\frac{1}{5}$ secs.

Second Gear (Ratio 7·3 to 1) 71 m.p.h. = 6,600 r.p.m. 13$\frac{1}{5}$ secs.

Speeds over measured Quarter Mile:—

Flying Start 83·35 (80·37) m.p.h. Standing Start 53·58 (52·95) m.p.h.

FIGURES IN BRACKETS REFER TO PERFORMANCE WITH 11 STONE PASSENGER

Braking Figures On SMOOTH TARMAC **Surface, from 30 m.p.h.:—**

Both Brakes 49 ft. Front Brake 56 ft. Rear Brake 86 ft.

Fuel Consumption:— ~~Town~~ 30 MPH 55, 50 MPH 46, 60 MPH 38 m.p.g. ~~Country m.p.g.~~

Oil Consumption:— 1850 m.p.g.

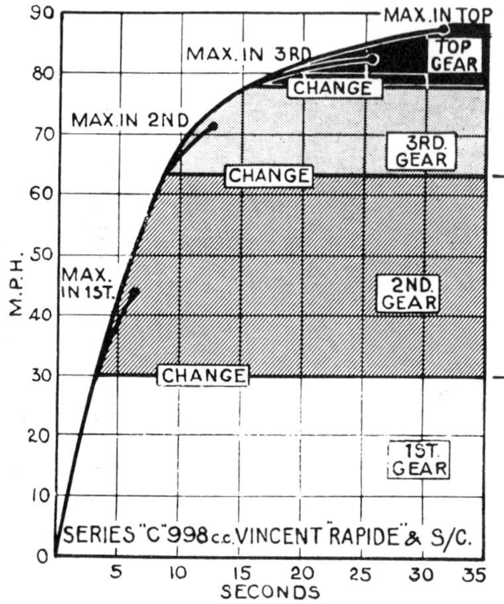

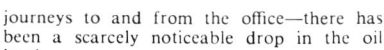

journeys to and from the office—there has been a scarcely noticeable drop in the oil level.

Mention of daily journeys introduces the subject of starting. It is making no unfair comment to say that earlier "Rapides" have been fickle in this respect. But 1951 modifications to the valve gear and cam contours have virtually "killed" that bother.

Knowing that the model handed over to *Motor Cycling* would come in for more than its normal share of hammering, the Vincent technical staff fitted comparatively "hot" Champion NA8 plugs instead of the standard N8s. Even so, there was little sign of plug-wetting or oiling and, generally, starting was a simple procedure. It was advisable to keep the air levers closed for the first minute or so, and to ease them open steadily, when starting from cold, but once the engine was warm, the mixture controls could be disregarded.

With more damping on the rear springing than would be required for solo use, and with the steering damper just biting, the outfit handled superbly, the weight of the sidecar only making itself evident by a suspicion of handlebar flap when decelerating below 40 m.p.h. The writer preferred the wide handlebars fitted to the standard short Vincent bars, but would have been even happier had there been a more definite backward curve in the bends. And being very long-legged, he would have liked to have had the footrests lower than the lowest level at which the standard range of adjustment permits them to be set.

From the passenger's point of view, the "Sherwood" gained full marks. Rear accommodation is sufficient to seat a five-footer or two small children in comfort, while the largest adult would not be cramped in the front seat. With the hoods in position, it is easy for the front passenger to get in or out without disarranging her hat. To say that the interior of the sidecar is snug in winter is true but, with only a small hood-flap to provide ventilation, it might become too warm if heavy rain necessitated complete battening-down in midsummer.

The suspension—rubber-bushed at the front end and on quarter-elliptic, multi-leaf springs at the rear—is such that there is absolutely no roll on corners and no unpleasant fore and aft pitching on bumpy roads.

Confirming previous experience on sidecar road tests, it was noted that the weight of a passenger had very little effect on performance figures—as little, in fact, as a mere $\frac{2}{5}$ sec. on the "flying quarter." It is the frontal area of the outfit which steals the m.p.h.—particularly over the "60" mark—and, undoubtedly, a contributory factor to the outstanding performance of the Vincent was the excellent aerodynamic contour of the "Sherwood" body.

With the machine costing £265, plus £71 11s. P.T., and the sidecar £106 2s. 1d., including P.T., making a total of £442 13s. 1d. the combination obviously comes into the luxury class. Yet at a glance at the tester's report sheet on this page immediately confirms that the Vincent-Blacknell outfit provides a performance, coupled with passenger comfort, which would cost many times that amount if the vehicle had a wheel at each corner instead of two in line and one at the side.

BRIEF SPECIFICATION

Engine: 50-degree vee-twin; bore 84 mm., stroke 90 mm., 998 c.c.; high-camshaft push-rod o.h.v.; dry-sump lubrication; oil tank capacity 6 pints; Lucas magneto ignition with automatic control; Miller 50-watt dynamo; Amal carburetters.

Transmission: Positive-stop four-speed Vincent gearbox with neutral selector; ratios 4.56, 5.47, 7.3 and 12.5 to 1; rear chain ⅝-in. by ⅜-in; ⅜-in. triplex primary chain with adjustable spring-blade tensioner.

Frame: Engine comprises frame basis; pressed steel top member, incorporating oil tank bolted to cylinder heads; pivot type, triangulated suspension at rear with adjustable shock-absorbers; front forks patent Vincent "Girldraulic" type with central spring and hydraulic damping.

Wheels: Fitted with Avon tyres, 3.50-in. by 19-in. front and 4.00-in. by 18-in. rear; twin 7-in. diameter brakes with compensated control, front and rear.

Tank: Welded steel 3¾-gal. fuel tank.

Dimensions: Wheelbase, 56 in.; overall length, 85½ in.; saddle height, 30 in.; ground clearance, 5½ in.; weight, 455 lb.

Finish: Black frame and tank, with gold lettering and lining; other parts chrome or cadmium plated or polished aluminium.

Price: £265, fully equipped, plus £71 11s. P.T.

Makers: Vincent-H.R.D. Co., Ltd., Stevenage, Herts.

THE SIDECAR

Chassis: Blacknell "Safety" of single main tube construction; quarter-elliptic rear springs, rubber bush front suspension.

Wheel: Mounted on stub axle with large-diameter taper roller bearings; Avon tyre, 3.50 in. by 19 in.

Body: Blacknell "Sherwood" child-adult single-door saloon, coachbuilt with aluminium panelling; folding backrest to front seat; luggage locker behind rear seat.

Dimensions: (See diagram) A = 81 in.; B1 = 54 in.; B2 = 20 in.; C1 = 38 in.; C2 = 32 in.; D1 = 19½ in. D2 = 18½ in.

Finish: All-black exterior with high-quality red leathercloth upholstery and fawn lining; separate roll-up hoods for front and rear passengers.

Price: Body £51, plus £13 12s. P.T.; chassis £32 15s. 4d., plus £8 14s. 9d. P.T.

Makers: Blacknell Sidecars, Ltd., New Nuthall, Notts.

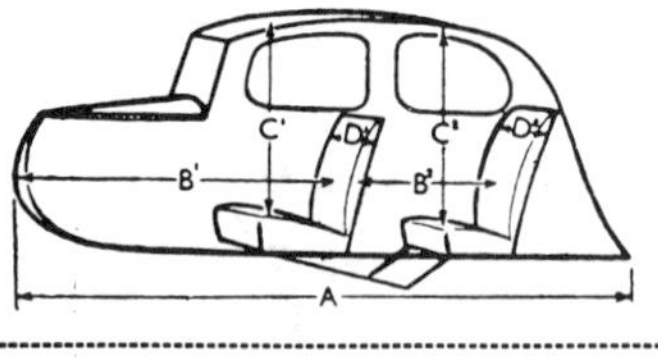

MOTOR CYCLING SPORTS MODEL ROAD TESTS

The 998 c.c. o.h.v.

VINCENT-H.R.D. "BLACK SHADOW"

A Hard-riding Pressman finds his Ideas of Fast Motorcycling Reformed

(Left) A group of riders survey the "Black Shadow" standing on the T.T. Course.

Do you remember the song and dance I created last year on account of having covered a measured quarter-mile in a shortage of time which equalled 112 m.p.h.? " Fastest standard machine in the world " I quoted and sat back with a complacent air completely belied by a readiness to mention my " fastest-ever " performance whenever the Tall Stories Dept. forgathered to exchange incredible yarns accompanied by pop-eyed wonder.

It was a Vincent-H.R.D. Series B " Rapide " that enabled me to claim intimate knowledge of the blurred landscape existing above 110 m.p.h.—and it was its creators, those same Supermen of Stevenage, who robbed my boast of its headline attraction by producing a *sports* edition based upon that touring tornado. This variation on a thousand-c.c. theme would be known as the " Black Shadow " and would possess a maximum in the region of 125 " per "—such was the gist of early Press notices. At which stage I ceased to marvel at my own previous daring dice and proceeded to lie doggo! Then, in mid-May, a brief note arrived which concluded, ". . . in the Island will be a ' Black Shadow ' for your transport and road test to follow. . . ."

By now, the highly individual specification which distinguishes a modern 998 c.c. Vincent-H.R.D. has been closely studied and keenly discussed by every bunch of road-burners. the world over. The specification panel deals briefly with general details and measurements of this extraordinarily successful 50-degree twin with its high camshaft short push-rod unit which produces such prodigious b.h.p., so let us dwell for a moment on the differences which make the " Shadow " faster than the previous fastest big multi.

Type 289 Amal carburetters of 1⅛-in. bore replace the more modest 1 1/16-in. Type G instruments of the " Rapide " and have bronze adaptors to suit. Pistons with a " bump " raise compression ratio from 6.8 to 7.3 to 1; ports, rockers and connecting rods are highly polished and triple-valve springs replace the duplex pattern. Bottom gear

becomes 7.25 in place of 9.1, while the gear cam-plate and clutch shoe carrier are drilled as an aid to swift " cog-shifting." Ribbed cast-iron brake drums in place of steel drums and Ferodo MR 41 linings to replace MZ offer reassuring anchorage on a new high level, of which more anon.

All engine components are specially selected for accuracy and fit in assembly, the Lucas magneto is laboratory tested and cylinder heads, barrels, crankcase and covers are " Pylumin " treated for paint adherence before receiving a stove-enamelling in lustrous black. The Miller electrical equipment features a 7-in. head lamp (in place of the " Rapide's " 8-in.) and a 50-watt output

dynamo of 3-in. diameter—this latter size will eventually replace the 3½-in. pattern at present standardized on the " Rapide." Finally, there is a Smiths speedometer of noble 5-in. diameter and most impressive 150-m.p.h. calibration.

It was Graham Walker himself who introduced me to the " Black Shadow "—with some typically candid comment anent our respective proportions. I found it somewhat of a strain to ride nonchalantly when permanently confronted by a " clock " with such ambitious figuring, and if you had seen the eager crowds which collected wherever the " Shadow " was parked in the Island you would have realized that modern man-

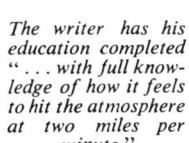
The writer has his education completed " . . . with full knowledge of how it feels to hit the atmosphere at two miles per minute."

MOTOR CYCLING SPORTS MODEL ROAD TESTS

hood has renounced Betty Grable as "essential to lasting happiness." So impressive are the zestful proportions of this latest space-pulverizer that my fellow North-countryman and B.B.C. favourite, Wilfred Pickles, was tempted to accompany me for a brief trip. And he thought "it were reet grand" too!

Following the convincing demonstration of Vincent-H.R.D. handling produced by the 1948 Senior Clubman's race, it would be superfluous for me to add any remarks on this score. Recently, in my report on the "Rapide," I wrote that "fast open bends could be tackled with a definite intention to stay on a chosen line . . ." and there is little need to add to the compliment in view of recent events. Once accustomed to the short bars a tendency towards "wander" at low speeds becomes minimized, but is always evident on initial getaway. Above walking speed there is no suggestion of conscious effort in piloting this 450-odd lb. of beautifully contrived metal exactly as required.

It took me a couple of days to get the starting drill fully organized but here I should interject that, when I took over, the machine had covered over 2,000 miles of gruelling test work. With two new plugs fitted (Champion NA8 type) the method from cold was: close both air levers, gently flood near-side carburetter, place right hand over intake of off-side carburetter and give three priming kicks of the well-proportioned starter crank. With the grip turned an infinitesimal amount a first-kick response could then be assured. "Hot" commencing required no special knack, but if the machine had been parked on its near-side prop for a short period it was found that the off-side carburetter tended to flood through the jet orifice, with a consequent spot of bother due to rich mixture.

The combination of a clutch somewhat "sudden" in action and a bottom gear ratio of 7.25 to 1 provided some startling getaways until I began to acquire the "feel" of things, but a little traffic-driving very quickly brought mastery. Two fingers are sufficient to control this ingenious self-servo clutch, which deals capably with all manner of abuse. Despite the need for generous revs. to obtain a smooth take-off in bottom gear it was possible to slow-march in top gear at 18 m.p.h. and to accelerate away in this 3.5 ratio from 22 m.p.h. Too much of this "plonking" technique did not suit the front plug, however, and is a practice neither desirable nor necessary, because all intermediate ratios are inaudible in use.

Weighing only 457 lb., the "Black Shadow" can be laid over in full confidence when cornering fast and steers to perfection.

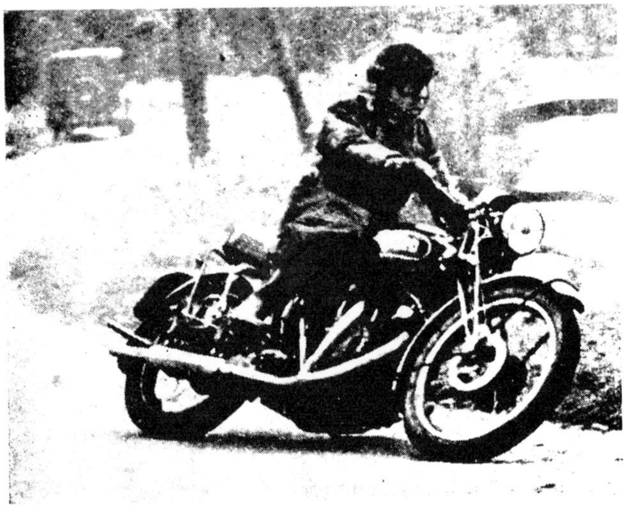

The question of gear changing brings two points of criticism—a tendency to "drift" out of gear on the over-run and a certain difficulty in engaging third at anything above 65 m.p.h. in second.

To state a definite cruising speed on the open road is well-nigh impossible, as the margin is set only by road conditions and the rider's capabilities. From a standstill to 100 m.p.h. acceleration is constant and colossal—there can be no other description—and in the course of a 362 miles-in-the-day test run I recorded an average I dare not print. A non-stop 270 miles, except for a very brief refuelling, was easily accomplished between lunch and tea—I never dine before 7 p.m.!

Such performances as this would be impossible or highly dangerous without a measure of braking capable of coping with two-miles-a-minute velocity. Take a peep at the test sheet and note that from 30 m.p.h. in top gear it is possible to stop in 22 ft. 6 in.! That I finished up seated on the filler-cap is hardly surprising, although it occasioned much mirth from two amazed witnesses. If there is anything more decided than the power of the Shadow's front and rear duo-braking I'm not sure that I want to experience it.

High-speed touring did not prove so hard on fuel as I anticipated, a state of affairs not difficult to understand when it is remembered that 60 m.p.h. in top gear means a mere whiff of throttle and no more than

MOTOR CYCLING

TESTER'S ROAD REPORT

MODEL 998cc. VINCENT H.R.D. "BLACK SHADOW."

Maximum Speeds in:— (Time from Standing Start)

Top Gear (Ratio 3·5 to 1) 122 m.p.h. = 5,485 r.p.m. 51 4/5 secs.

Third Gear (Ratio 4·2 to 1) 110 m.p.h. = 5,935 r.p.m. 32 1/5 secs.

Second Gear (Ratio 5·5 to 1) 91 m.p.h. = 6,429 r.p.m. 15 3/5 secs.

Speeds over measured Quarter Mile:—

Flying Start 120·2 m.p.h. Standing Start 61·9 m.p.h.

Braking Figures On DRY TARRED **Surface, from 30 m.p.h.:—**

Both Brakes 22½ ft. Front Brake 31 ft. Rear Brake 38 ft.

Fuel Consumption:— 51 m.p.g.

Oil Consumption:— 1,500 m.p.g.

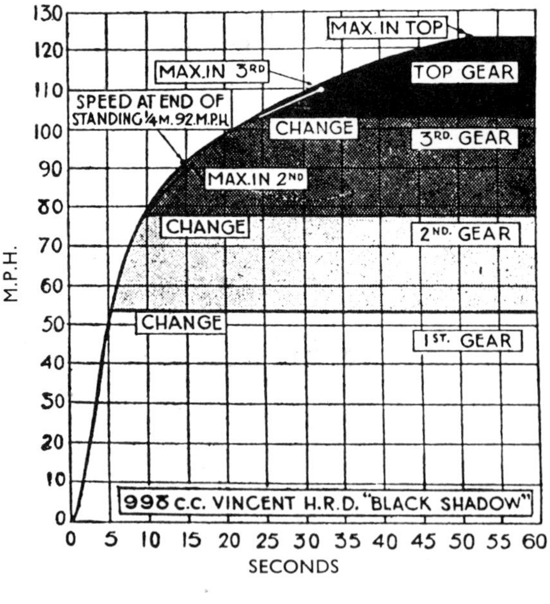

MAX. IN TOP
MAX. IN 3RD
TOP GEAR
SPEED AT END OF STANDING ¼M. 92 M.P.H.
CHANGE
3RD. GEAR
MAX. IN 2ND
CHANGE
2ND. GEAR
CHANGE
1ST. GEAR
998 C.C. VINCENT H.R.D. "BLACK SHADOW"
M.P.H.
SECONDS
0 10 20 30 40 50 60 70 80 90 100 110 120 130
0 5 10 15 20 25 30 35 40 45 50 55 60

MOTOR CYCLING SPORTS MODEL ROAD TESTS

" Pin-up " for any motorcyclist. The sleek compactness of the machine makes an attractive picture.

Navigator's bridge. The short handlebars, with their nicely placed controls, are features of the " Black Shadow." Note the dual carburetter air levers, the 5-in. 150-m.p.h. trip speedometer and the oil filler projecting through the fuel tank.

2,700 r.p.m. On long-distance runs the tank would barely accept three gallons after 178 miles of mixed going and 75-80 m.p.h. cruising with the wind astern. This easy and effortless travel brought a lively problem concerning other road users who frequently misjudged the Shadow's rate of approach, due to the lack of noise and fuss. There was hardly more than a smooth burble from the exhaust, and although the valve gear could be detected at work it never reached annoying cadence.

Vibration was not apparent at any engine speed, the most that was felt being a faint tremor at peak revolutions in second gear. Pinking was evident and clearly audible if liberties were taken with the throttle, and it *real* acceleration were required from speeds as low as 50 m.p.h. it was kinder to employ the 4.2-to-1 third gear.

No doubt smooth power output is contributed to largely by the impressive rigidity of the engine unit with its deeply spigoted cylinder barrels and sturdy crankcase dimensions—a power plant which guarantees speed plus long-term reliability. Which reminds me to apologize to the makers for having worn a " flat " on the clutch cover due to a certain heartiness in " laying 'er over " in the course of high-speed cornering!

Full marks are awarded to such features as adjustable spring-frame damping, exceptional range of footrest adjustment (and the rear brake pedal follows suit), the Feridax Dualseat with sliding tool-tray, tommy-bar wheel fixing and the means to adjust the rear chain without use of spanners, two propstands in addition to a stout rear stand, hand-adjustable brakes and fork damper, steering which never required the damper at all, an indicator-cum-hand control for setting the " cogs " to neutral or as required, and a stout pair of hinged scrapping or pillion rests. In short, a machine designed and built by riders for those who ride hard, far and fast.

And now, with full knowledge of how it feels to hit the atmosphere at two miles per minute, I go to compose a new song-and-dance routine. . . .

BRIEF SPECIFICATION

Engine: 50-degree twin-cylinder o.h.v.; 84 mm. bore by 90 mm. stroke = 998 c.c.; compression ratio, 7.3 to 1; crankshaft carried on roller and ball bearings on drive side and roller on timing side with outrigger roller journal; nickel-chrome connecting rods mounted on triple-row needle-roller big-end bearings; alloy cylinder barrels with shrunk-in cast-iron liners; alloy heads; high camshaft short push-rod all-enclosed valve gear; triple valve springs; polished ports, rockers and connecting rods; dry sump lubrication by reciprocating and rotary plunger pump with pressure feed to valve gear; separate Type 289 Amal carburetters, 1⅛-in. bore with bronze adaptors; forward-mounted, gear-driven Lucas magneto—laboratory tested; all engine components specially selected on assembly for accuracy and fit.
Transmission: Unit construction four-speed foot-operated gearbox with gear indicator; ratios 3.5, 4.2, 5.5 and 7.25 to 1; self-servo operated clutch; ⅜-in. triplex primary chain with externally adjusted spring-blade tensioner; aluminium oil-bath

chaincase; rear chain ⅝-in. by ⅜-in. roller with finger adjustment; gear cam plate and clutch shoe carrier drilled to facilitate high-speed gear changing.
Frame: Engine unit comprises frame basis; pressed-steel member containing 6-pint oil tank bolted to cylinder heads and supporting fuel tank; pivot-type triangulated suspension at rear with adjustable shock absorbers and enclosed springs; front forks, girder pattern, with central compression spring and shock dampers.
Wheels: 26-in. by 3.00-in. front tyre ribbed and 26-in. by 3.50-in. rear studded pattern; hubs of light alloy with Skefko taper-roller bearings; brakes, Vincent-H.R.D. dual type balanced and compensated 7-in. diameter by ⅞-in.; ribbed cast-iron drums with Ferodo MR 41 linings; both wheels quickly detachable with tommy-bar spindle nuts; mudguards of polished duralumin; spring-up prop stands each side and rear stand with tommy-bar fixing.
Fuel tank: 3¾ gal. capacity stainless steel

Dimensions: Wheelbase, 56 in.; overall length 85½ in.; overall width 25½ in.; saddle height, 30 in. (unladen); ground clearance 5½ in.; weight 457 lb. (dry).
Finish: Small parts cadmium plated; exhaust pipes, silencer, wheels etc., chromium plated; tank, black with gold lettering and lining; frame members, black enamel; heads, barrels, crankcase and covers treated by " Pylumin " process (for paint adherence) and enamelled black.
Equipment: Miller 6-v. 50-w. separate dynamo (3-in.) driven from primary chain; 7-in. headlamp and rear lamp incorporating stoplight; electric horn; special 150 m.p.h. Smiths speedometer with 5-in. dial, internal front wheel gearing; Feridax Dualseat incorporating tool tray; pillion footrests.
Price: £300 plus £81 P.T.
Extra: Double sprocket rear hub, price £2 7s. 6d. plus P.T.
Makers: The Vincent-H.R.D. Co., Ltd., Stevenage, Herts.

Super Profile

OWNER'S VIEW

The first interview was with Frank Oliver, a motorcycle enthusiast of many years ago who is perhaps representative of many owners in having left motorcycling for some years, and then returned choosing one of the bikes they remember well. Frank's Shadow is kept in very smart condition and possibly like most Vincents is run to ride and rally, but not used as daily transport.

PB: Why did you return to active motorcycling, and why with a Vincent?
FO: I had always liked Vincents, I used to run a Vincent when I was riding in competitions; I took that to Australia on a tanker. I'd always been interested in motorcycle sport but I was always falling off. Then I went on to cars. (Frank was quite a successful driver in car rallying). Then we came to live here... one of the builders said he knew me and offered me a ride on his bike up on the hill. Trying that bike I thought 'God it's great to be back on a motorbike again'. Then shortly afterwards I was ill and felt I needed something else, a Vincent was always something I wanted to get again. I knew Jim Jennings, and went round to see him. He had a Comet so I bought it from him. He had a Shadow he didn't want to sell, but when he came round to

see the Comet after it was done up he was so impressed that he took it back in part exchange against the Shadow.
PB: What sort of problems have you had with this one?
FO: You know the clutch trouble (Frank had sought advice on his clutch problem, which had proved to be the result of an assortment of incorrect parts, assembled in the wrong order, and held together with split pins, wrong thread screws etc.) One of the problems is I'm no engineer. Eventually I had a problem with the clutch and as we were due to go to the French Rally, I 'phoned up the spares company and Jane said she would send off the bits I might need without my having to send the old bits first. My mates were in hysterics because as advised I got a sheet of paper and as I took the bits out I made pencil marks and put the bits down on the paper. And that's how I put it back again, just reversing the process. Apparently I've got a mixture of Series 'C' and 'D' parts and cannot use the correct gasket, so I did exactly as told and bunged it full of RTV silicone gasket and did up the nut. Just minor troubles with the electrics. Although the system looks like Miller, it has been altered and is basically a Lucas dynamo and regulator. The only other difficulty has been with the headlight, which has packed up on a couple of occasions. But I've fiddled around with the wires and got it going. Apart from that the only other trouble has been carburation. One carburettor was very badly worn so I've replaced it with one from a Comet. At first the bike wouldn't run properly but I've gradually got it right and starting better.
PB: What is your general opinion on the spares availability, and the help you get?
FO: Although the bits and pieces I've needed haven't been of great importance, the actual response I've had from the spares people has been incredible. I have phoned them up, usually in a rush, on a

Thursday, often with only a vague description of what I need. Usually the bits are on my doorstep the following day, or on the Saturday. There is never any hassle. I don't think you can ever beat service like that.
PB: How do you feel about the Vincent Owners Club?
FO: The people that I know in the club I regard as my friends. There is a lot of talk about name badges, and I think it is here that something is lacking. The senior officers of the Club assume that everyone is one of the 'family' as it were. I'm in selling and it is always bad to assume the customer knows the product you are selling. It pays to show him what he is getting and what he might be missing. Except in the case of their particular friends, I feel the Club officers are a little bit aloof. That suits me as a person, but I do understand the people who write in and say they feel left out in the cold.
PB: That is probably a good point. Is it worth while for people who feel that way to persevere?
FO: I think they should.
PB: I ought to get you to say a bit about the bike. How enthusiastic are you about it? I see in the garage a new four cylinder BMW and the Vincent; you have got rid of everything else. Will the Vincent be staying?
FO: Oh it's got to stay. A Vincent Shadow represents something to me, I wouldn't get rid of it unless I had to and that would be a sad day.
PB: Does it live up to its reputation, even with the faults we have talked about?
FO: The faults I've had I think are just plain bad maintenance, and lack of ability on my part. For riding it is a very comfortable machine, its got long legs, and I love riding it. It doesn't compare with the BMW, but I don't think it should, because it comes from a different world; there is no reason why it should, because it is 30 years out of date. It is magic to me. One thing I love about it is going to the British Bike Show in Plymouth, where a lot of

youngsters' interest in the Vincent and other old bikes is incredible. I think one sad thing is they are now so expensive. If they were more readily available there would be a lot more youngsters taking interest.

The second interview was with Alan Jennings of Braunston, Northants, whose Rapide and Watsonian Palma sidecar outfit is regular transport for Alan, Judy, and the two children.

PB: Can you tell me why you got a Vincent, and how it has served you?

AJ: In 1973 I was working on an RAC-ACU training scheme and met Chris Reeve. I'd had a Velo and he said what I needed was a big Vincent and took me to the club. One day he said he knew where there was a tatty one and we went to see it. I was very disappointed to find it in a thousand pieces. Never having had a Vincent and seeing how complicated it looked, I wasn't interested. But around the back, under a tarpaulin, was a Vincent with dustbin fairing, flat tyres etc. We put petrol in, fiddled and bumped it and it started, so I bought it in 1974 for £425. Within a week I was pleased because I'd got it running. I had needed to get a petrol tank for it, and it had no lights, or dynamo so I had to scrounge around. I ran it for two years, then I needed a sidecar. I acquired this one for £50, after talking to a man at a Dragon Rally. I visited him, tied it on and rode it back. Unfortunately, the sidecar proved too much for it and the big end went, so I had the engine down. There was a tide-mark across the big end and the engine, which is why it went. I was told it was probably the original, even though the mains had been changed.

Mine is a Series B, 1947 engine number 99, but in 1962 the frame was changed to Series C specification with Girdraulics added, whether just to update it or because of an accident I do not know. The main problem was oiling up so I took off the cylinder heads and put in new valves and guides which improved it. The other problem you read about is the clutch and it got to the point where quite literally I couldn't pull away once or twice. Then I went on my first long run, to a conference. Every 70 miles or so I stopped for a stretch, and it proved most embarrassing to have to drain the surplus oil from the chaincase which was coming through the mains. So I adopted the dodge of drilling a hole back into the engine, which helped, but obviously the problem was a sign that the clutch was getting tired. Then the big end went and the engine had to come down. All the faults I found were the normal faults that are well known, like jumping out of first gear due to incorrect adjustment. All the other faults were due to fair wear and tear.

I found the bike to be quite economical really. I did the 1975 ACU National Rally and averaged 64mpg over 600 miles which is jolly good. With a sidecar on we get about 40mpg which is also pretty good when you hear about figures like 25mpg. I've always had galloping oil consumption.

PB: You have made a dynamo modification.

AJ: I found that as I drive quite a lot at night I got through three secondhand dynamos in two years, so I wanted a cheap conversion. I was going to fit an alternator but was advised against it for various technical reasons, so I just bought an ordinary Lucas 12 volt car dynamo. I made a dummy mounting the same diameter as the original dynamo, and then overhung the shaft and used an 'A' sized pulley, removed the battery to make room for the car dynamo and adjustment, and put the battery in the pannier. I've run that 12 volt system for over six years and it's only just now that the bearings are starting to go. It might look Heath-Robinson but it works well and allows one to convert to the original headlamp size, using a Wipac unit and a 60 watt quartz-halogen bulb, and to run indicators which is essential in modern conditions. The other mod I did because I go touring and so have a top box and panniers, which makes it extremely difficult to use the rear stand. So I made a home-made Series 'D' stand, having looked at others but not having one to copy. It has been fine although with the longer 'Petteford' sidecar springs it doesn't quite lift the rear wheel clear of the ground and I have to put a bit of wood under it to remove the wheel.

PB: You started off with the Owners Club, then got the bike, rather than the other way round. Any comments?

AJ: Oh yes! I certainly enjoy being in the club, although sometimes you feel that some people have been in the club for so long that you're on the outside. I particularly like the foreign rallies. In fact we've been abroad on the sidecar outfit six times; to Holland twice, right up to Hamburg and back, toured Brittany on it, to Luxembourg, Belgium (Judy interjects "and three German rallies"), mostly with two children. One thing we have found at some of these rallies is that a lot of men are even older than I am (Judy interjects again "even older" with a laugh). They have all got families, but they don't take them. You find at a lot of rallies there are a lot of blokes, but few families, not as many as I'd like to see one of the main reasons being that not everyone likes sidecars. We often go enormous distances and find ours are the only children there.

John Waltham, a Dorset lad, was reluctant to be interviewed because he felt that he would not be able to be objective, but that is surely normal amongst motorcyclists whose marque loyalty can be very strong. John is very well qualified to talk about Vincent twins having owned a 'D', a 'C', and an 'A' in that order.

PB: How is the 'A' going?

JW: I've just had it rebored, and the oil consumption is beginning to settle, from 60 miles per pint it is now over 160, although as I run it up to 80 or 90 the oil leaks have started again. It's going quite well, but I'm biased. If it rattled and fell to pieces I'd still be pleased with it. In many ways it is comparable with a modern bike, in some ways superior, and of course in many ways inferior. A friend of mine with a Suzuki 1100 rode it. He got it into top at 30 and wondered where the other gears were, then opened the throttle and found all that torque. The handling is not bad, but it will never match anti-dive and Marzocchis, yet for its day it is not a bad handling bike at all.

PB: You had a 'D' first, which you did not keep long, then later you decided to get another Vincent?

JW: I bought the 'D' because I wanted a Vincent, which was the ultimate, but I got this thing which hadn't been well maintained and I reaped the whirlwind of it. Everything was so far out of adjustment it was just a pain. It did prove rather unreliable but as I was only 17 or 18 I didn't have much motorcycling knowhow. The 'D' as I remember it didn't handle particularly well after the Enfield I had before, which I thought was quite reasonable, but it was probably well worn. If I had known what I know now, it would have been put right.

I came to the 'C' reluctantly, just because it ought to be a good sidecar hauler, probably the only British bike other than a Brough, which was getting harder to buy. I got the thing and never turned back. The 'C' I thought was a really good bike. I covered an awful lot of miles on it, solo and sidecar. It really served me excellently, its big end eventually failing when travelling at 100mph with a sidecar on, chasing a Honda Four! I put another big end in it, and I did 5,000 to 10,000 miles per annum on it for a number of years when it never failed to get me home. I wouldn't have parted with it except that I wanted an 'A' Rapide.

The first day I saw Harry Cox's Series 'A' I knew I was going to have one, and I spent years searching and asking. Eventually I bought this Rapide from Bill Hancock, after it had been apart for 16 years. At first I just put it together to see how it went; it took Mandy and I to France last year. Then I put in the new big end it needed, home brewed to my own specification, and now a rebore. In cold daylight it probably isn't as good a bike as the 'C', although I think some of the steps after the war were retrograde. The frame spine bolted to the engine is always claimed to be an advantage, but it is a disadvantage when it comes to cylinder head removal. The 'A' is a perfectly practical bike really, as long as you can go places in wellies! It has the sheer complexity of looks and the performance of 100mph on a machine 46 years old, but retard the ignition and it chuffs around as a vintage bike. Now I've got one I have achieved my motorcycling ambition. Life holds nothing more for me!

BUYING

About 12,000 Vincents were made, including the 500cc singles. A few still turn up abandoned, in barns, but most purchases are made on the open market. Advertisements appear in the weekly and monthly motorcycle press, as well as the club magazine *MPH* available to Vincent Owners Club members. All Vincent twins command a high price as 'classic' machines, the enclosed Series 'D' and racing Black Lightnings especially because of their rarity. A Black Shadow has more 'charisma' than a Rapide, so tends to command a slightly better price. In truth there is little difference, for the majority of both models now run on 7.3 or higher compression ratios, with more modern carburettors of similar sizes, and the selected cams have probably been replaced or built up in the intervening years. The ribbed brakes of the Shadow are worth having, the 5 inch speedo and engine number of the Shadow attract many. A few enthusiasts prefer the Series 'B' with its girder forks as the machine feels lower and lighter, but the Series 'C' is much less rare, and still boasts a 30 inch seat height as standard.

All Vincents are now at least 30 years old, and it is an optimist who expects one to have survived so long without serious wear or, worse still, damage from abuse. It may have been properly repaired, 'bodged', or still be suffering, for a Vincent will keep running with some appalling treatment. There are, unfortunately, more people in the world able to produce a beautiful appearance than there are good mechanics who understand a Vincent clutch or can shim a crank. Those who have the time and mechanical ability might do well to buy as cheaply as possible, budgetting to rebuild to their own standard as soon as possible. This approach should be viewed with caution; many is the rebuild which has taken many years, or has never been completed. Others must look as critically as they can on a prospective purchase, seeking advice from the more experienced, and still being prepared for an unexpectedly large repair bill at a later date. The story is not so discouraging if this realistic approach is made. The new purchase may turn out completely sound from the beginning, and if not, any problem can be solved, any part found. When a Vincent is well put together it will stay that way for a very long time and give very good service, as can be seen from some of the long term road-tests published.

The more common engine problems are loose spindles and worn cams in the timing case, loose rocker bearings (which tap but do no harm), misaligned flywheels leading to loose main bearings, stripped exhaust port threads, and worn engine shaft shock absorbers and shafts. The gearchange is adjustable; selection problems may be simply the adjustment, but be sure they are not due to a broken camplate spindle boss, or stripped gears, because these are expensive to repair. Note that the gearbox can be fully dismantled without splitting the cases. Ordinary wear and tear on valves and pistons is easily taken care of with readily available and modestly priced spares. Vincents are notorious for clattering 'like a gas stove dragged over cobbles', and so some rattle is to be expected. They should not knock, or whine, or leak oil, except from breathers and dampers. There are plenty of inspection caps through which examination can be made. The only major area of wear in the cycle parts, apart from tyres, chains and brakes, is in the front forks where spindles, bushes, and eccentrics do wear. Modern stainless items are longer lived than the original, not least because they do not generate a grinding paste of rust and oil. Wheel and swinging arm bearings are almost indestructible taper rollers. Ball cup and cone steering head bearings on a Vincent are no better or worse than those on most other motorcycles; steering will probably benefit from their careful replacement. If the electrics are original, the magneto may be tired. It is quite likely the dynamo or regulator will not work, and lighting may be poor. There are specialists in all these areas, willing to repair anything 'back to standard', or sometimes to a more modern standard. This should be preferred to the use of over- or under-size repairs.

Many of the modifications likely to be found are useful and well proven over the years.

Brakes: Ribbed drums, stiffened balance beam support. Some prefer twin cables, less spongy but requiring much stronger hands. Set up properly, the brakes are good, but few are set up this way.

Suspension: Koni dampers do not leak like originals, but new ones are too hard on the front. Longer rear springs may be used, and a fully sprung seat. All of these improve pillion comfort considerably; those with short legs may find standard fittings more suitable.

Carburettors: Unworn, the original separate float chamber types are sound carburettors, although one side dribbles on the engine when the sidestand is used. Unworn left-handed (front) ones are hard to find although it is possible to have them reclaimed. Many machines have been converted to later Concentric MkI or MkII types. 28mm or 30mm at most is advisable for ordinary use.

Ignition: V-twin magnetos should be fitted with automatic advance and retard, and platinum points for good sparks at the odd angles required by the 50 degree cylinder angle. Nevertheless tungsten points have proved adequate even with manual control (which eliminates the hard to get ATD). With a good magneto and carburettors, starting should be satisfactory, but will deteriorate if the latter are out of tune. Many owners convert to coil or electronic ignition for easier starting. This does, however, increase the burden on the generator.

Electrics: Even in its heyday the Vincent was criticised for lighting not up to its performance standards. The passing years have not improved the standard parts. Converting the dynamo to use a Lucas regulator improves reliability. Modern light units are better than the originals, but 6 volt bulbs bigger than 36 watt ask too much of the standard set up and glow dimmer, especially with coil ignition. Thicker wiring is a better way to good lights. 12 volt electronic conversions are commercially available, and neater than the addition of belt driven alternators. Dynamo power output is increased significantly, as long as the engine is revved freely, and permits the use of much improved quartz halogen lighting.

Wheels: 20 inch tyres are only available in batches, and in a very limited range of patterns. Many riders forego the lightness of steering and fit smaller diameter wheels, usually the touring sizes fitted with more modern tyres often in 'low profile' form. Speedometer accuracy is slightly affected.

Stainless: Whenever possible, and economic, stainless steel was used as standard on the Vincent. This trend has been taken further over the years, many parts being readily available only in these steels. Thus stainless cap head screw sets and nuts replace the original cadmium plated steel cheeseheads.

CLUBS, SPECIALISTS & BOOKS

Clubs

The Vincent-HRD Owners Club (VOC) was formed in 1949 and enjoyed good relations with the manufacturers when Vincents were in production. The strength of the club can be judged from its ability to launch an independent company for the manufacture of spare parts when this became necessary. The newcomer probably will be primarily interested in the accumulated knowledge of many years available by personal contact, through publications such as the club magazine *MPH*, supplied monthly, or from the club's Technical Service Officer. The club also offers a very full social calendar of rallies, race meetings, dinners etc. and includes a number of branches overseas. Families are usually catered for at events, and even if the new member finds that it takes time to fall in easily amongst the longer standing friendships they should be assured that all Vincent owners, even of the humblest cyclemotor, are welcome.

Membership Secretary: Adrian Cattell, 67, Sintin Avenue, Allenton, Derby.

Information Officer: Cyril Malem, 8 Telford Road, Ferndown Industrial Estate, Wimborne, Dorset, BH21 7QL

Specialists

Spares are manufactured by the VOC Spares Co., the Holders, Maughan and Sons, and others, and are freely available from a number of retail outlets:

Conway Motors, 224 Tankerton Road, Whitstable, Kent, CT5 2AY.

The VOC Spares Co. Ltd., The Wharf, Burford Lane, Lymm, Cheshire.

W.E. Humphries Ltd., 123 Essex Road, Islington, London N12SN.

Grays Motorcycle Centre, 63 Southend Road, Grays, Essex.

C.D. Hollis, The Square, Main Street, Claypole, Newark, Notts, NG23 5BA.

Maughan and Sons (Precision Engineers), 42 Townend, Wilsford, Nr. Grantham, Lincs, NG32 3NY.

Maughan and Sons also provide full repair and reclamation services.

Cams and followers can be reclaimed by **Gary Robinson,** Hi-Profile, Cranmore Ave., Cranmore, Isle of Wight, PO 41 OXS. For magneto and dynamo overhauls (and Vincent repair work) contact **Dave Lindsley,** Elton Vale Works, Elton Vale Road, Bury, Lancs. This list is not exhaustive, and other names and addresses, or details of other services may be found by consulting the motorcycle magazines. These addresses are correct at the time of going to press, but should always be checked as they are sometimes subject to change.

Books

A number of books which the owner/rider/restorer will find valuable are available through the VOC, or spares stockists. These include:

Vincent Motorcycles (by Paul Richardson, the Service Manager)

Spare Parts List (exploded diagrams, part names and numbers)

Instruction Sheets (factory service sheets)

Riders Handbook

Know Thy Beast (a book compiled by a club TSO, including details of many well-proven modifications)

Vincent-HRD Motorcycles. Available from **Bruce Main-Smith Retail Ltd, PO Box 20, Leatherhead, Surrey,** originally written by him for 'Motor Cycling'

There is also a selection of books available to interest the enthusiast and historian:

The First Vincent Scene Bruce Main-Smith Retail Ltd.

Vincent-HRD Gallery Roy Harper, Vincent Publishing Co.

Vincent-HRD Story Roy Harper, Vincent Publishing Co.

Vincent, fifty years of the Marque P.C. Vincent, Vincent Publishing Co.

P.C.V. The autobiography of Phillip Vincent P.C. Vincent, Vincent Publishing Co.

Vincent Vee Twins Roy Harper, Osprey.

World Motorcycles: Vincent-HRD Peter Carrick, Patrick Stephens.

George Brown, Sprint Superstar Cliff Brown, Haynes Publishing Group

Many titles by P.E. Irving (Tuning for Speed, Black Smoke, etc.) also contain references and detail to his work at Vincents. The last three titles from the list above are also readily available from Bruce Main-Smith Retail Ltd, and with the Vincent Publishing Co. titles from Roy Harper.

PHOTO GALLERY

1. Gordon Duerden's Series 'C' Vincent Black Shadow
looking very much as it would have done in the
showroom, beckoning to its first owner.

1

2

2. Some of the men behind the Vincent, pictured at the Montlhéry record-breaking in 1952. Left to right: Timekeeper, John Surtees, Robin Sherry, Danny Thomas, H. Reynolds, K. Mainwaring, Ted Davis, Johnny Hodgkin, Ken Bills, Dennis Lashmar, Phillip Vincent, Clement Garreau (French importer), Vic Willoughby, Paul Richardson, Cyril Julian.
(photo: Ted Davis)

3. In 1925 Howard Davies won the coveted Senior TT on his new HRD. Thereafter the Vincent-HRD marque carried this winged 'figure of Mercury' copied from the TT trophy. This version, seen on the top of the petrol tank, is one of 5 variants, with wording suitable for 1949-53.

4. Matching tank transfer is this Vincent scroll, which superseded the initials HRD in 1949.

5. On tank transfers and inspection caps the name is THE VINCENT, but cast on the engine it is simply VINCENT.

3

4

5

6. John Hurt's concours 1951 Series 'C' Rapide.

6

7. In 1946 an all alloy, unit-construction engine-gearbox was very unusual. A drive-side view of the Rapide shows the resulting clean lines and oiltight chaincase.

7

8

9

10

8. The polished timing cover, gearbox, oil and exhaust pipes prove so attractive that many owners convert their Black Shadows into White Shadows with a similar finish!

9. Another novelty for 1946 was the one-piece dualseat. More comfortable than the old pillion pad, especially when that was bolted to an unsprung mudguard, it was also much neater than the pre-war Vincent-HRD arrangement of saddle and linkage-mounted pillion seat.

10. A 1939 Series 'A' Rapide stands in front of two single cylinder Comets of similar vintage. This Australian Rapide was supplied originally with an engine in racing trim. (photo: Author)

11

12

13

11. Vincents incorporated many 'rider features', the best known of these being the easy rear wheel removal, without tools. Lowering the rear stand also releases the hinged mudguard, which may be raised out of the way.

12. The mudguard hinge is a sturdy, and highly polished, aluminium casting.

13. No need for spanners, the spindle has a tommy bar, the brake rod engages 'motion blocks' which are slotted to pull out by hand, and the torque arms have spring-loaded clips (the clip is obscured by the rear stand here). Even the chain will then slip off without dismantling its spring link.

14. As an optional extra, the reversible rear wheel could be fitted with two sprockets. Thus gearing could be changed between solo and sidecar ratios with ease.

14

15

16

15. The 'Girdraulic' front fork was designed with consideration for sidecar work too. The bracing against sideloads of the girder fork principle is superior to that of a telescopic fork.

16. At the top of the springbox, each side, is this eccentric. Turning it half a turn simultaneously moves the lower link pivot, thus reducing trail, and increases the spring preload, suitable for use with a sidecar.

17. Owners often wish to check engine and frame numbers, which may be used to trace original details from records held by the Owners Club. The frame number appears on the steering head, and here on the left rear fork lug.

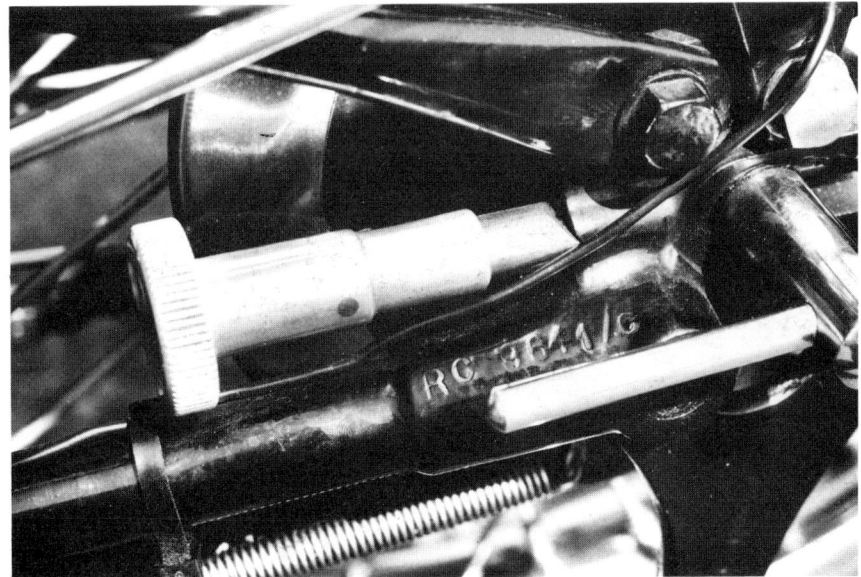

17

18

19

20

21

18. Below the front cylinder, on the left side, is stamped the engine type code (F10AB), model (1), and number.

19. Some very early engines still exist. Surviving in Australia this HRD embossed crankcase has engine number 4!

20. Also still existing is the actual Black Shadow featured in the original roadtest. JRO 102 is in extremely original condition, and in this view can be seen the early Series 'B' specification, including Brampton girder fork, and the early pattern gearchange linkage – ball jointed to follow footrest adjustment. (photo: Author)

21. JRO 102 is seen here using one of the two prop-stands, left and right side, provided as standard. (photo: Author)

22

23

22. PAL 709 is a Series 'C' version of the Black Shadow theme, differing from the 'B' primarily in its suspension, with the Vincent-designed Girdraulic front fork.

23. Comparing similar views of JRO 102 and PAL 709 accentuates the very compact nature of the original design.

24

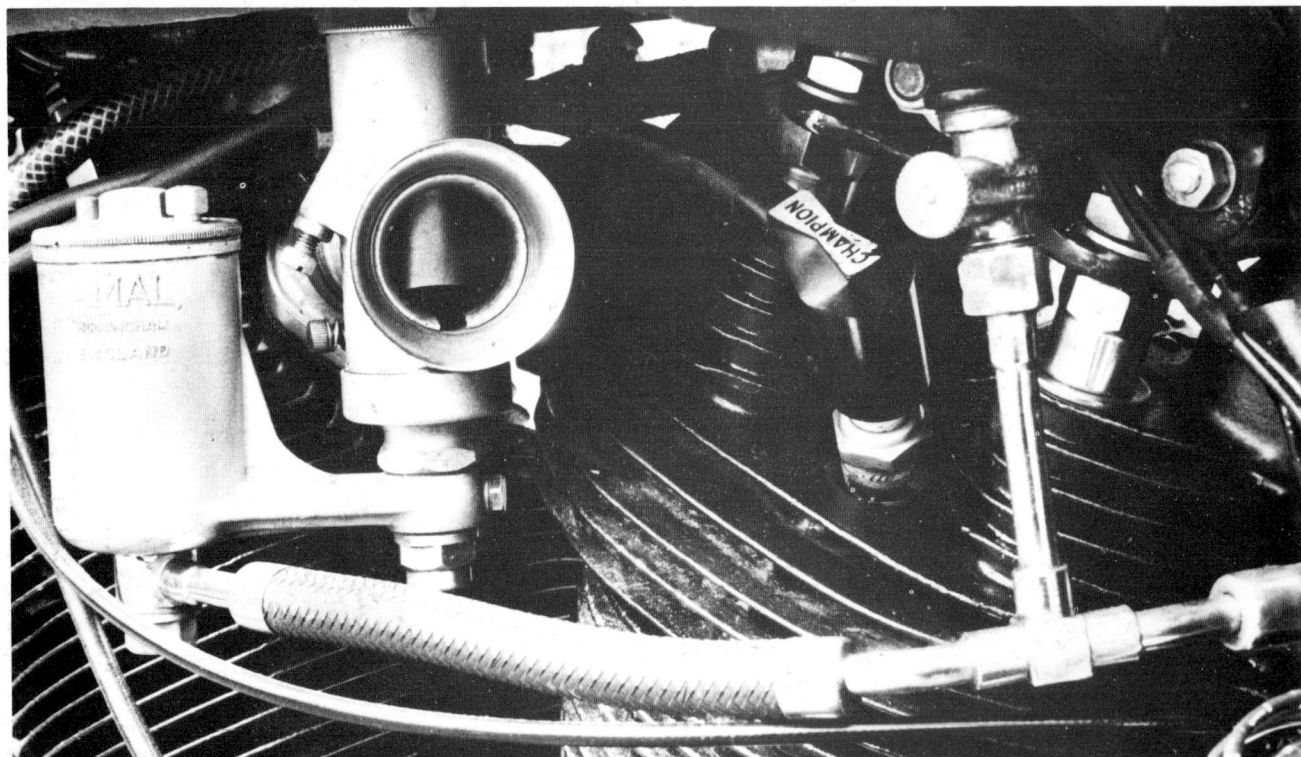

25

24. There is not much room to spare around the rear carburettor; adjusters are fitted in the cable runs, not the carburettor tops, to ease the cable curve.

25. The front carburettor needs a cutaway in the tank above, but is otherwise not cramped. Early models, however, had the adjusting screws inaccessible on the inner side, until Amal produced this version, first in brass, then later when demand increased, in a zinc-based diecasting.

26. Ted Davis's Black Shadow shows the tyre pump carried in the lugs provided under the petrol tank. (photo: Ted Davis)

27. The 50 watt Miller electrical system was the best specification available from the British Industry in 1946, but Vincent owners of the day soon complained that it was inadequate for their machines.

28. The Miller cartridge regulator is very compact, but not very sophisticated, and it is extremely difficult to set up. Most regular riders convert either to a Lucas 6v unit, or to a modern electronic 12v conversion.

29. The distinctive STOP-tail rear light, which was adequate in the early 1950s, but is now illegal in standard form. Hidden internal modifications can overcome this, but after-dark riders are well advised to fit something bigger and brighter.

26

27

29

28

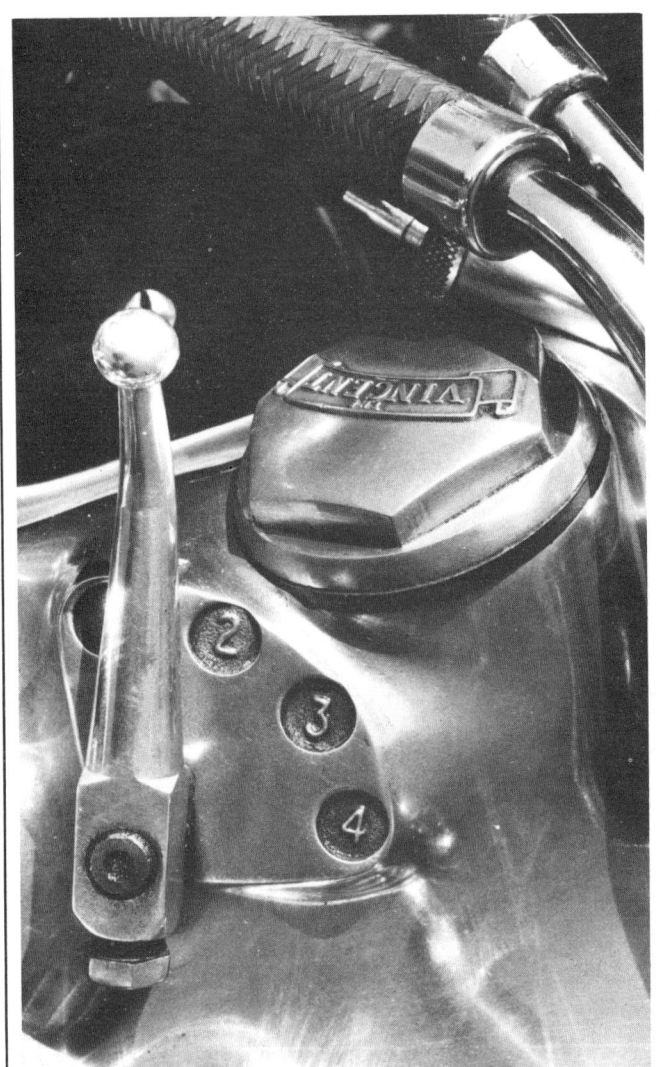

30

33

30. The external gear indicator, which also has uses during maintenance, and can even be used to overcome failures of the positive stop or gear location mechanisms when out on the road.

31. Pride of place on the Black Shadow goes to the 5 inch diameter 150mph Smiths speedometer, mounted directly in front of the rider.

32. The prototype 5 inch diameter speedometer for comparison, showing that development included clarifying the markings. The standard, black handlebars, are fitted with the factory control layout, left to right: clutch (lever hidden), exhaust valve lifter, dip-switch, friction steering damper knob, twin choke levers, horn button, front brake (lever hidden) and throttle twistgrip. (photo: Author)

33. The Rapide rider has only the normal 3 inch diameter speedometer, calibrated to 120mph. This handlebar has yet another lever on the left. It controls the manual advance-retard, non-standard but very often fitted.

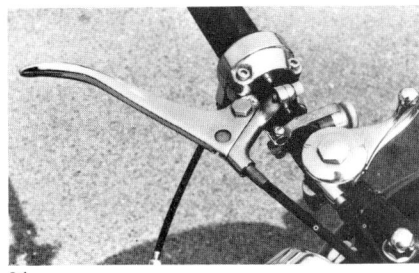

34

35

34. *Original levers did not have the safety feature of ball-ends. Restorers should also note that there are two standard dimensions for the spacing of the cable nipple from the pivot, and use of the wrong one adversely affects control operation.*

35. *Twin brakes were fitted, front and rear (until the Series 'D' reverted to a single rear). These are the ribbed drums of a Black Shadow, stiffer and better cooled than the plain Rapide variety.*

36. *This 'balance beam' transfers the same force to the right brake as the cable applies to the left. Adjustment of cables, balance beam stop (the slotted screwhead), and brake levers is critical for achieving braking distances as in the roadtests.*

37. *Rear brake efficiency is affected by the footpedal adjustment; pivoted on the footrest it follows any change in footrest position. Rubbers were embossed HRD until 1949, VINCENT thereafter.*

36

37

38. Hard rubber-cased 'black' batteries like this are now difficult and expensive to obtain, but it is possible to put a small modern battery inside a scrap original one.

39. An inspection cap is provided for checking primary chain tension, adjusted with the bolt just visible under the chaincase bulge. Chaincase oil level is checked with the bolt directly under the inspection cap.

40. Gearbox oil is checked with the dipstick underneath this cap over the chaincase.

38

39

40

41

41. Above the clutch dome is this small cover. Although the sprocket it reveals seems larger than the hole, nevertheless it is designed to come out, if required.

42. Col Crothers modified his Series 'B' Rapide to take Australian speed records up to 175mph on Lake Eyre. (photo: Author)

42

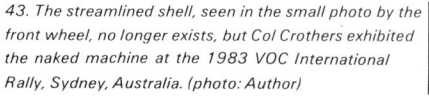

43

44

43. The streamlined shell, seen in the small photo by the front wheel, no longer exists, but Col Crothers exhibited the naked machine at the 1983 VOC International Rally, Sydney, Australia. (photo: Author)

44. Finger-operated chain adjusters are another easy maintenance feature. A telescopic end, engaging with a V-notch, permits equal adjustment either side simply by counting clicks.

45. Attention to detail is indicated by the provision for these balance weights on the wheels.

46

46. The early, complicated, gear-linkage was not popular and the factory soon copied private owners with this directly-mounted lever, retaining adjustment by the provision of alternative footpiece holes.

47. Under the saddle is carried a tooltray. The little bracket is a useful modification, allowing it to be padlocked into place for security both against theft and accidental loss if loose in its runners.

48. Under seat and tooltray are the rear suspension springs, housed in telescopic covers. Series 'C' models have a single hydraulic damper mounted between the two springboxes, as seen here.

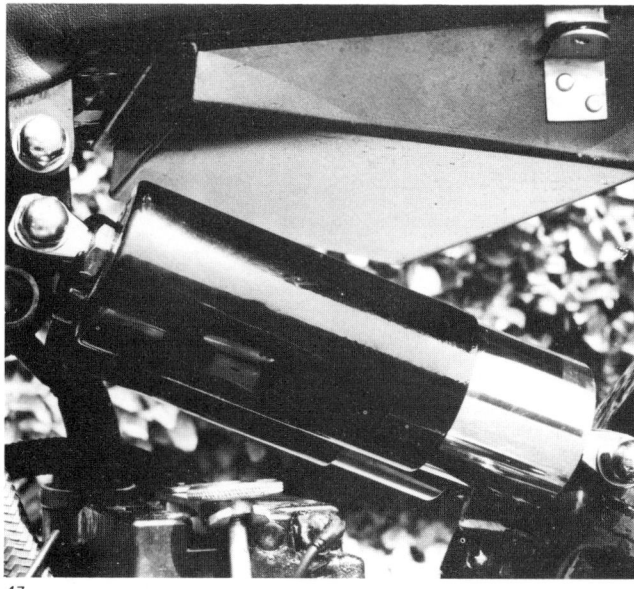

47

48

49. A link either side mounts the dualseat directly to the unsprung rear frame, but its angle is chosen to provide approximately half springing for the pillion seat. This compromise was dictated by fashion.

50. Also incorporated in the seat stay is a friction damper, the only damping provided on Series 'B' models. The alloy knob permits the rider to adjust the damping.

49

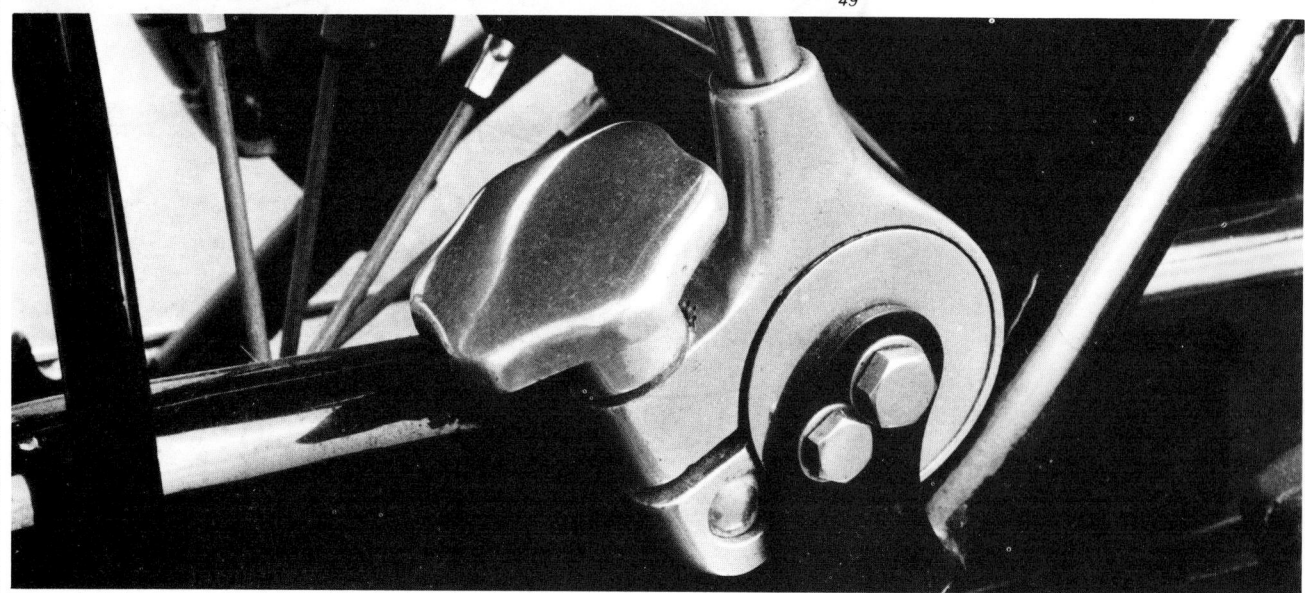

50

51

52

51. The Girdraulic fork also features two springs in telesopic tubes, long soft springs either side.

52. The single, Vincent-manufactured front damper, is in the middle of this busy area in front of the steering head.

53. The wheel turns a full circle. Fritz Egli manufactured lightweight spine frames with conventional twin damper swinging arms. Terry Prince in Australia has developed this version, with single damper 'modern cantilever' rear suspension. Just like the original! (photo: Author)

53

54

55

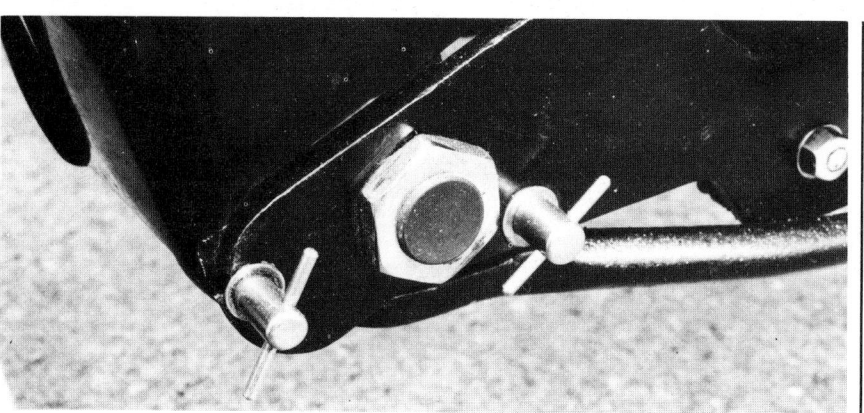

54. Prop stands may not look strong, but do not bend.
They sometimes do not reach the ground, and at other
times sink into soft tarmac so that a little block of wood
is a favoured Vincent accessory.

55. The front wheel spindle, like the rear, has a stainless
tommy bar for ease of maintenance.

56. Undoing these two nuts converts the twin
propstands into a front stand, to lift the front wheel.
Hexagon heads, requiring spanners, are standard, but
owners often carry the factory policy of fitting stainless
tommybars further.

56

57. A special lower front sidecar mounting had to be designed because of the lack of any frame members. This hollow axle accepts a long stud and eyebolt.

58. The use of stainless steel, as original equipment, is seen here in the brakerod, motion block, stoplight spring anchor, and wheelnut (which is lipped and must not be turned with a spanner).

57

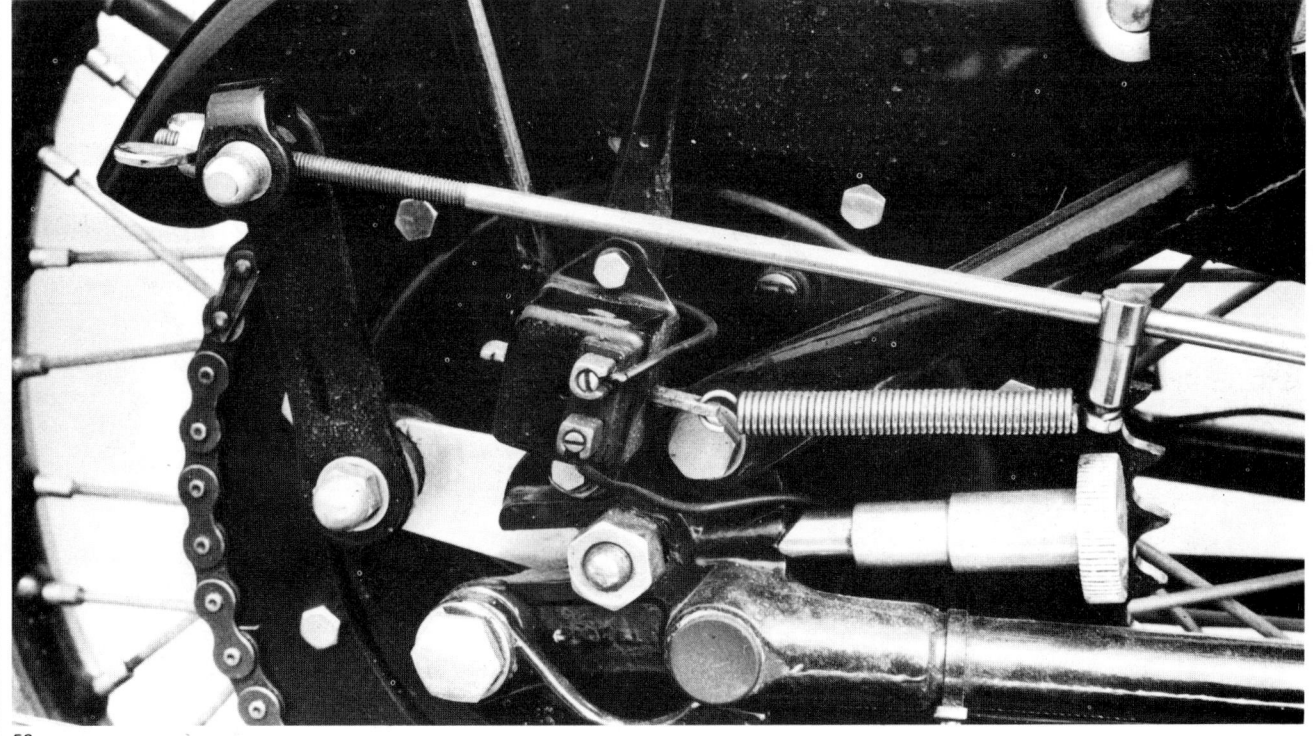

59

60

59. In 1949 a sidecar was listed in the factory catalogue, but it was simply a bought-in item, not of Vincent manufacture.

60. Ex-factory personnel pictured in 1979, left to right: Alan Rennie (assembly), Arthur Barlow (Toolroom), Murry Crickman (Toolroom), Phil Irving (Design Engineer), pre-war rider, Ted Davis (Development Engineer).

61. Ted Davis also campaigned this Black Lightning sidecar outfit very successfully in 1952/3. Here he is seen establishing the 88mph lap record at Boreham circuit. (photo: Ted Davis)

62. Valvecaps are not positively locked, but do not come loose. Some owners like to pick out the lettering with paintwork, as here.

63. When finned exhaust nut castings were short, this alternative type was machined from bar. The fine threads are visible, and patience in fitting is needed if they are not to be cross-threaded.

61

62

63

64

65

64. The polished, close-fitting water excluder rings keep rain out of the brakes. The right-angle speedometer gearbox has a grease nipple, to be used with care.

65. A rare sight enjoyed by the Author. Reset to zero on acquisition, the mileometer completed a 'circuit' in less than 10 years.

66. With 250,000 miles to its credit, PUB 335 has some justification for looking scruffy. Viewed alongside a 30 year younger machine, the Vincent design shows its compactness. (photo: Author)

66

67. The heart of a Vincent is the V-twin power unit. This sectioned 1951 Rapide engine shows clearly the geardriven camshafts, straight forked rockers, and the resulting short pushrods. (photo: Science Museum)

68. The short, straight handlebars, lead to a little heaviness in town, but give excellent steering at higher speeds, and are often known as 'HRD straights'.

69. Rear view. The STOP lamp was all the average contemporary motorcyclists could expect to see of 'The World's Fastest Standard Motorcycle'!

67

68

69

C1

C2

C1. This well-cared-for Rapide is owned by John Hurt of Broadstone, Dorset. It is a Series 'C' model, featuring hydraulic damping of the suspension, and Vincent's own Girdraulic fork.

C2. The Rapide has a few modern fittings, such as the battery and a sensibly sized rear lamp. With the exception of the chromium chainguard, which originally would have been black enamelled, the brightwork is similar to standard.

C3

C4

C5

C3. The all-alloy power unit offers plenty of scope for polishing. The Series 'C' had separate float-chamber type 276 carburettors as standard: Amal Monoblocs, as fitted here, were not adopted by the factory until 1954 on the Series 'D' models.

C4. Four widely splayed pushrod tubes rise from the timing case, which contains two high camshafts. Above the tubes are four inspection caps which reveal the tappets. It is possible to withdraw the pushrods and the forked rocker assemblies through these inspection points.

C5. Pre-war and early post-war V-twins usually had a rearward facing exhaust on the back cylinder. The two forward facing pipes, coiling around the timing cover, are a distinctive feature of the Vincent design. The inspection cover nestling between the two sweeps gives access to the magneto drive, for timing purposes.

C6

C7

C8

C6. Gordon Duerden, of Nailsea in the South West of England, can exercise this Series 'C' Black Shadow on the winding country roads which run across the background of this scene, or on the modern motorways which now run close by.

C7. PAL 709 probably shines a little better even than when it was brand new, but it remains very close to its original specification, even down to the tiny STOP lamp.

C8. Centrepiece of a Vincent V-twin is the engine unit. To distinguish the sports version of the Rapide, an unusual black finish was applied to the engine. This gave the model its name, originally 'Rapide, Black Shadow model', but soon known simply as the 'Black Shadow'.

C9

C10

C11

C9. The famous 'Shadow Clock', a 5 inch diameter 150mph speedometer prominently placed for easy reading at the speeds available on 'The Worlds Fastest Standard Motorcycle'. The black handlebars are quite correct; Vincents did not normally fit chromium-plated bars.

C10. The Vincent-HRD Company displayed the HRD monogram prominently in the pre-war and early post-war years, with 'Vincent' written only in small letters on the tank transfers. In 1949 this was revised and thereafter the engine and petrol tanks displayed the name Vincent.

C11. Colour photography is almost wasted on the black enamel, aluminium, and stainless steel of a Vincent. Gold leaf lining and transfers on the petrol tank, however, complete the traditional black-and-gold favoured by many quality marques.

C12

C13

C14

C12. In 1946, when the post-war design entered production, separate gearboxes were still the choice of most designers. The clean lines of the unit-construction Vincent engine-gearbox are particularly evident in the drive side profile.

C13. Compact dimensions for a 1000cc machine were obtained with the frameless method of construction. The rear fork pivots directly on the rear of the gearbox, and the steering head is attached to the top of the engine, thus there are no frame tubes around the engine.

C14. The steering head and oil tank bolt together underneath the petrol tank, to form a frame spine. In this close-up are seen the head brackets, retained by the cylinder head nuts, and the two bolts which hold the spine to them.

C15

C16

C15. The Rapide model name was adopted for the first 1000cc V-twin models introduced at the 1936 Motorcycle Show. This timing side view of a Series 'A' Rapide shows the frame tubes, exhaust, and oil pipes which gained these models the unofficial name of 'the Plumbers' Nightmare'. (Photo: Author)

C16. The final variants of the 1000cc V-twin Vincents were the 1955 enclosed Series 'D' models. This line includes touring 'Black Knight' and slightly more sporting 'Black Prince' versions of the theme. (Photo: Author)

C17

C18

C17. Some people's tastes are not catered for by standard models, especially a generation after they were made. The machine in the foreground is fitted with a purpose-built 'Egli' frame, featuring conventional pivoted fork rear suspension and a telescopic front fork. Behind it is a modified machine utilising the standard Vincent rear suspension and Girdraulic fork, but with seat mounting and fittings to the owner's taste. (Photo: Author)

C18. This modernised Vincent-HRD twin, fitted with a telescopic front fork and fully-sprung seat, has also been 'Lightningized' with rear-set footrests, twin open exhaust pipes, no lights and other features of the racing models. It is based around a 1949 machine, which is 'new' compared with the 1926 HRD 70/S standing behind. The 70/S is a 500cc sidevalve from Howard Davies' Wolverhampton factory. (Photo: Author)

C19. Concours judge at the 1977 VOC Shadow Lake Rally was the late Paul Richardson, Service Manager at the Vincent works in the 1950s, and author of the invaluable handbook more popularly known by his name than its title 'Vincent motorcycles'. Also in the picture, in a white tee-shirt, is American importer Eugene Aucott. (Photo: Author)

C20. Vincent-HRDs from many countries were ridden, flown, trailered, or used combinations of all three, to attend the first Vincent-HRD Owners Club International Rally held at Shadow Lake, Canada, in 1977. (Photo: Author)

C19

C20